FAMILY WORSHIP
FOR THE REFORMATION SEASON

OTHER AVAILABLE TITLES FROM THIS SERIES

Family Worship for the Christmas Season

OTHER PROJECTED TITLES FROM THIS SERIES

Family Worship for the Easter Season
Family Worship for the Summer Season
Family Worship for the Thanksgiving Season

FAMILY WORSHIP

FOR

THE REFORMATION SEASON

Ray Rhodes, Jr.

Solid Ground Christian Books
Birmingham, Alabama USA

Solid Ground Christian Books
PO Box 660132
Vestavia Hills AL 35266
205-443-0311
sgcb@charter.net
www.solid-ground-books.com

FAMILY WORSHIP FOR THE REFORMATION SEASON
Ray Rhodes, Jr.

First edition printed in August 2008

Cover design by Borgo Design, Tuscaloosa, AL
Contact them at **borgogirl@bellsouth.net**

Scripture references in this book are from the New
King James Version of the Bible.

ISBN: 978-1-59925-189-9

Dedication

This book is dedicated to my best friend and lovely wife Lori. She is a virtuous woman who loves our Lord, manages well our home, joyfully cares for our children and delights in her husband. She is also a significant contributor to this book by her writing, ideas and support.

In Memory of My Grandparents

Raymond and Pauline Rhodes
Lint and Elsie Smith

Special Thanks

Special thanks to my daughters; Rachel, Hannah, Sarah, Mary and Lydia. They are a delight to my life. Life is good in a house filled with lovely and gifted ladies that surround my life with beauty, music, romantic movies, and much laughter.

Thank you to Ray and Dorothy Rhodes (my parents) and Rodney and Lou Webb (Lori's parents) for their encouragement and love through the years. Thanks as well to all of our brothers, sisters, nieces and nephews and their families.

Thank you to my editors; Lori and Rachel Rhodes and David Bailey.

Thank you to Grace Community Church that so kindly accepts a Pastor who is scattered about with many responsibilities.

Thanks to the Lord for providing the following people and places that were instrumental in my writing.

Amicalola Falls State Park Lodge and Conference Center, Dawsonville, GA. My dear wife gave me a two night stay at the Lodge hotel to write. The kind folks at Amicalola Falls allowed me usage of their lobby on several occasions. The view is breathtaking (www.amicalolafalls.com).

Georgia Baptist Conference Center, Toccoa, GA. Thanks to director Bill Wheeler and Georgia Baptists who provided me with a two night stay. This is a wonderful place to visit, write and eat (toccoa.gabaptist.org).

Shepherd's Refuge, Cleveland, GA. Special thanks to my Swiss friends Ruedi and Sandy Mettler who provided numerous days and nights for me to retreat with my wife and to write. Ruedi and Sandy are lovely people, and new and treasured friends. (www.shepherdsrefuge.org).

Disclaimer

As you read this book you will note that some characters, places and themes receive significantly more attention than do others. You will also find that some very important figures of the Reformation were either left out completely or received only scant attention. Due to time and space I could not include more of the story of the Reformation. I am greatly indebted to, and leaned heavily on, most of the books that are listed in the bibliography. I commend them to you for your study. When dealing with the facts of history I have not attempted to footnote as the data is common to most books on the subject. I have made choices when there are disputes over the spelling of names and dates of characters. I have sought to be accurate. Likeness to any other book is not intentional. The characters of the Reformation (like those of any other time period) were sinful people. They are not the heroes. God is the hero of any good work that has come through His servants.

Table of Contents

How to Use This Book

This book contains thirty-five daily devotions/ activities. Scan the entire book before beginning and you will find information both earlier and later in the book that will be helpful. Feel free to adapt the studies and activities to your family. Before leading a session read the section for the day. Note any materials that you may need for the family activity. There are some items that you will use time and again—like a globe or book. It would be a good idea to keep those items handy. There is a materials list near the end of the book. Not only will you have opportunity to learn more about the characters and theology of the Reformation, you will also learn more about the geography of the Reformation. If you have a map you might want to highlight key places and pray for the spread of the gospel in those areas.

The lessons are simple. Read the passages of Scripture and the text of the study. Join in the family activity and pray. Most lessons can be completed in fifteen minutes.

The book can be used at anytime during the year. Consider starting the book on October 1st as you work towards Reformation Day on October 31st. Or you might start on October 31st and work through November.

A Perspective from Lori Rhodes

For many people the significance of October 31st is related to the Halloween celebration. However, in recent years our family has given attention to the events that were set in motion on October 31st 1517. That was the date that Martin Luther nailed his 95 theses to the church door and the Reformation began.

After years of trying to ignore Halloween and a half hearted effort to learn what the Reformation was all about, I set out with more intent to discover the Reformation. The more I read the more amazed I became. There is a world of history interwoven in the lives of godly men and women whose calling was to stand on the Word of God. As I begin anew to teach my children what it means to rely on the Bible, I will be including lessons of these great heroes of the faith from the Reformation era.

As you read your daily family devotion, take a few minutes to write down a short biographical sketch of one of the heroes described in the day's reading. You will note some additional characters in a list near the end of the book. Roll the writing up as a scroll and tie it off. At the end of the month, bring your family together and reread the scrolls.

We used hard paper and twine to make the scrolls a little more authentic, but you can be as simple or creative as you would like. Gather the scrolls in an old basket and keep in a prominent place as a reminder to continue your devotions and to build excitement for your family's end of the month reading. As your children learn to tell the story of a Christian hero they are more likely to remember it for years to come.

Our family gathered with our church last year to read from such scrolls around a huge bonfire. As we read aloud stories of those drowned for their beliefs about baptism or burned at the stake for the gospel, the glow of the fire was a stark reminder of the Reformer's costly faith and endurance. It was so meaningful to sit with like-minded believers to recount the investment of our Christian forefathers. We are the beneficiaries of their faithfulness.

Thoughts on Family Worship

The Reformation era left a rich legacy of teaching on family worship. The goal of family worship is for you and your family to be exposed to the character of God so that you may know and worship Him. Family worship involves regular family gatherings and will always include Scripture readings and prayer. However, as this book illustrates, you may also use other material that will help you to focus on the great work of God throughout history. Remember, as the Puritans taught us, your home is a "little church" where Christ is to be worshipped. The little church does not replace the local church; however, faithfulness in family worship will greatly enhance the congregational worship of God.

Family worship is worthy of your attention. Though in this book you will read primarily of the influence of the men of the Reformation, you should also know that women were essential in the progress of the Reformation. Women were and are also vital to family devotion.

The Puritan Thomas Manton, in the introduction to the Westminster Confession of Faith, tells of the importance of women in family worship and management:

> "Especially women should be careful of this duty; because as they are most about their children, and have early and frequent opportunities to instruct them, so this is the principal service they can do to God in this world... And doubtless many an

excellent magistrate hath been sent into the Common-wealth, and many an excellent pastor into the Church, and many a precious saint to heaven, through the happy preparations of a holy education, perhaps by a woman that thought herself useless and unserviceable to the Church. Would parents but... labor to affect the hearts of their children with the great matters of everlasting life, and to acquaint them with the substance of the doctrine of Christ, and, when they find in them the knowledge and love of Christ, would bring them then to the pastors of the Church to be tried, confirmed, and admitted to the further privileges of the Church, what happy, well-ordered Churches might we have!"

Manton encouraged the usage of the Westminster Catechisms and Confession in the instruction of children. In this spiritual treasury we have a systematic diet of sound doctrine and instruction.

Truly our homes are to be "little churches," schools and seminaries. Fill your shelves with good books and introduce them as friends to your family. Look for opportunities throughout each day to point out the awesomeness of God displayed in all that He has created. Gather with your family regularly for more specific study of the Bible, the reading of biographies, prayer and singing.

Introduction

Family Worship for the Reformation Season

Scripture Reading: Mark 11:12-24

On Monday morning of the week in which Jesus would be crucified, He and his disciples travelled from Bethany towards Jerusalem. Jesus was hungry. In the distance He saw a fig tree clothed with leaves. The leaves signaled that there would be fruit on the tree.

However, upon arriving at the tree, a discovery was made. There were no figs.

Several years ago a new restaurant opened in our town. One evening I decided that my family and I would have dinner there. However, upon arriving we saw a sign on the door, "Restaurant closed: Out of food." The building was still there. However—the purpose of the restaurant, to serve food, was not being fulfilled. We had to find our nourishment elsewhere.

This is somewhat like the fig tree. The fig tree had all of the indicators of fruit but there were no figs.

As a result, Jesus could not alleviate his hunger at the tree.

Jesus did something very interesting. He cursed the tree and predicted that it would never again produce fruit. The next day the tree was withered from the roots to the top.

When Jesus cursed the tree He was condemning the nation of Israel for not producing the fruit of true faith. All around were the "leaves" of religion. There was the city of Jerusalem with the gold and marble covered temple at its center. The temple was so beautiful that travelers described it as a snow capped mountain. A portion of the temple was called "the court of the Gentiles." In that area people from all nations could gather to learn about God and pray. God had ordained that the temple be a "house of prayer for all nations."

Jesus approached Jerusalem which had, during this Passover season, over a million visitors. He could see the sprawling temple complex on its thirty-five acres. The temple represented the worship of the Jewish people and hope for the nations. What Jesus found at the temple was "worship" that had been perverted. Jesus condemned the fruitlessness of Israel by cursing the fig tree and He condemned the worship of Israel by cleansing the temple of those who had turned it into a "den of thieves." The cleansing of the temple was exemplified by Jesus turning over the tables of the money changers.

God commands His people to be fruitful and to engage in true worship. The religious leaders of Israel had failed in both points.

The Reformation was a time during which the fruit and the worship of the religious establishment were soundly condemned. Religious activity had replaced faith in Christ with faith in the Church. Financial abuse had saturated the established religious life and the ordinary people of the day had been deceived and robbed by their leaders.

During the Reformation false religious practices and worship forms were exposed and condemned. We might say that the fig tree of the religious system was denounced and the tables of the religious leaders overturned.

The result was that God brought a great revival to the people and the church has never been the same.

Buckle your seat belt for a month long adventure into some of the key characters and themes of the Reformation.

PART ONE

Major Characters and Places of the Reformation

Day One

Providence in the Life of Luther

Scripture Reading: Proverbs 16:9; Romans 8:28-30

The providence of God refers to God's care for and direction of all that He created. There are no accidents. The Reformation was a rediscovery by Christians of the greatness of God and His providence over everything.

In order to understand the Reformation it is essential to get to know Martin Luther. God's providence is evident in the life of Luther in a number of ways.

1. *Family.* Luther's dad wanted him to be a lawyer and provided for him to be educated in law. Though Luther never became a lawyer, there is no doubt that his training was used by God to help him develop a sharp mind.
2. *Weather.* When I was a boy I had a gripping fear of thunderstorms. I needed to learn

more about God's providence. God's superintendence (providence) over all things (including thunderstorms) illustrates both His care and purpose. God's purpose for all that He created is that everything and everyone bring glory to Him (Colossians 1:15). One day while Luther was travelling a violent thunderstorm erupted. Luther was frightened. His fear was more over his perception that he was under God's judgment than of the thunderstorm itself. Luther cried out to Saint Anne (considered to be the patron saint of the miners), "Help me, Saint Anne, and I will become a monk." Luther would later realize that praying to anyone other than God is futile. He also later believed that he sinned by becoming a monk. Nevertheless he would eventually give God glory. God used the monastery as a means of bringing Luther to the gospel.

3. *Travel.* An out of town visit can leave a lasting impression on a person's life. My oldest daughter Rachel recently went on a mission trip to Honduras. While there, she came to know some needy people who lived in an area appropriately referred to as "the dump." Her trip is likely to have a lasting impact on her life. While Luther was at the monastery his conscience was often troubled. He was fearful because he was vividly aware of God's holiness and his own sinfulness. This led Luther to long hours of

confession that left him frustrated and even angry at God. Luther felt for a time that he hated God. Johann von Staupitz had oversight of Luther and encouraged him to visit Rome. His trip to Rome left him deeply troubled over the state of the Church. He found astonishing hypocrisy and abuse of power. Perhaps Luther recalled Jesus entering the temple and finding the perversion of worship and the extortion of the common person. Luther's trip planted seeds that would grow into his official protest against the corrupt practices of the Church.

4. *Theology.* Luther received the Master's and Doctorate degrees. His studies led him to read with great interest the writings of Augustine which pointed him to the teaching of the Apostle Paul. As we shall discover this study became the key that the Lord used to bring comfort and clarity to the heart of Luther—but first there would be more struggles.

5. *Printing Press.* Just prior to the Reformation the printing press was invented. Therefore when Luther nailed his 95 theses to the church door it was printed and widely distributed. The Reformation, in God's providence, spread quickly due to the printing press.

6. *Marriage.* Luther discovered that Church teaching on celibacy for priests was unbiblical. The Lord provided a runaway

nun by the name of Katharina von Bora for Luther—they were married on June 13, 1525 and had a large family. Luther called his wife Katy and she was a great encouragement to his work.

Family Activity

Take some time to consider the providence of God in your family. Discuss certain events or people that God has used in your family for His glory. Make a "Providence Journal." The purpose of a providence journal is to record God's provision of people, events (even suffering), and material possessions. As you record God's providence thank Him that He is watching over and directing your steps. Over a period of several days complete a reading of the book of Esther and underline how God's providence is evident in the key characters.

Prayer

Lord we thank You that though we make our plans, You are directing our steps. Help us to find comfort in Your providence over our family and all things. Amen.

Day Two

The Morning Star

Scripture Reading: Psalm 19; Mark 1:1-8

As a boy I would often gaze into the sky at night. I was amazed at the beauty of the stars and the vastness of the universe. Just before sunrise the morning star is visible. It is an indicator that a new day is about to begin.

Prior to the Reformation the church was in a dark period. During those days a morning star rose on the scene. His name was John Wycliffe. His life and ministry was as a morning star indicating that the day was about to break and the sun would soon shine. The sun indeed would rise in the characters of Martin Luther, Ulrich Zwingli, John Calvin, and others.

John Wycliffe, from England, is called the "morning star of the Reformation." He was a faithful student of the Bible, a powerful preacher and a godly man. He preached against the wickedness of religious leaders and against the corruption that he saw in the church. Wycliffe is most remembered for his work of translating the Bible from Latin into English. Getting the Bible into the language and hands of the common man was one of the significant works of Wycliffe and of the Reformers. What must be remembered is that Wycliffe did not have the benefit of the printing press and so his work was hand copied. Can you imagine how difficult and time consuming it would be to write out the entire Bible by hand?

Wycliffe was often persecuted in his ministry. He died in 1384.

Richard Newton writes, "He was buried in the graveyard connected with his church at Lutterworth. About 44 years after his death, his enemies dug up his bones, burnt them to ashes, and threw the ashes into the Swift. Thomas Fuller quaintly said about the Swift River, that it 'conveyed his ashes into Avon; Avon into Severn; Severn into the narrow seas; they into the main ocean. And thus the ashes of Wycliffe are the emblem of his doctrine, which now is dispersed the entire world over.'" (See *Heroes of the Reformation*" by Richard Newton, p.3, published by Solid Ground Christian Books)

Family Activity

Who is a person that has had a major influence in your life? Maybe a family member, pastor, coach or teacher? Why do you admire them? Have each member of your family name such a person. Write down their qualities. Consider giving some of the folks on your list a call. Ask them who it was that influenced them. Some of the most recognizable names in history were preceded by some lesser known person who helped to pave the way. John Wycliffe is indeed "famous" but not as much as Martin Luther. However God used Wycliffe to impact the Reformers who would follow him. God used John the Baptist to pave the way for Jesus. Have your children hand-copy several verses of the Bible. Ask them how long they imagine it would take to copy the entire Bible? Remind them that is what happened during the time of Wycliffe.

Prayer

Lord thank You for the people that you have used throughout history who have prepared the way for others. Help us to remember that we stand on the shoulders of those who have gone before us. Amen.

Day Three

Luther at the Door: Part 1

Scripture Reading: Acts 5:31, 13:38, 26:18;
Ephesians 1:7; Colossians 1:14

October 31, 1517 is a day that Christians around the world remember because that is the day that Martin Luther nailed his 95 theses to the Church door in Wittenberg and the Reformation began. The 95 theses would spread through the land like wild-fire because, as we have already learned, in God's providence the printing press had been invented.

When we think of Martin Luther we imagine him red-faced with hammer in hand fiercely pounding his protest document to the door of the Castle church. In reality the church door was sort of like a community bulletin board where announcements were made and issues discussed. In the case of the 95 theses, however, Luther's message spread far and wide and found a path all the way to Pope Leo. Leo was not impressed. Leo considered that Luther was acting like a drunken man and would eventually sober up and see things more clearly. Luther was not a drunk, but he *would* see things more clearly—increasingly he would view things from a biblical perspective.

At the heart of Luther's 95 theses was the Church's teaching on indulgences. Indulgences came from the time of the Crusades during which people were persuaded to go to war, with the promise that they would receive spiritual blessings granted by the Church. Luther believed that neither the pope nor the church had power to convey forgiveness of sins from a "treasury of merit" that was maintained by the church.

Nevertheless the pope, having wasted much of the church's resources, was in need of more money for his building projects. Johann Tetzel came up with the idea to establish what we might call an indulgence road show. Indulgences would be sold and the people would be motivated to purchase them. Manipulative sermons and outrageous promises were made by the indulgence preachers. A typical indulgence sermon contained statements like these: "Can you hear your dead relatives screaming out in pain in purgatory while you fiddle away your money?" The theology of purgatory taught that there was an intermediate state between heaven and hell where unresolved sin issues could be settled. According to Catholic dogma, one could not be assured of salvation until the end of their lives. Only then could it be determined if the person had sufficient merit to go to heaven. If not, and the person had committed no eternal sin, then off to purgatory they would go. Purgatory was not a place of ease. The church offered false hope to folks whose hearts were heavy over the plight of their loved ones. The church offered a way for purgatory to be shortened or even for one to be released from purgatory. Help was offered through the selling of indulgences (certificates) which bore the signature of the pope.

Tetzel came up with a little rhyme that served as a means to teach his false doctrine.

> *When a coin in the coffer rings*
> *A soul from purgatory springs.*

Playing on the emotion of people who were basically ignorant about the Scriptures, church leaders were able to secure large sums of money to fund the building of St. Peter's Cathedral.

Luther thought that if the pope were aware of the charlatan practices of men like Tetzel, certainly he would take action to remedy the situation.

Luther was sadly mistaken on this point.

Family Activity

Find a container that could be used as an offering plate. Have your children place coins in the plate. Then ask them the question; "If we give this money to our church, will giving the money cause anyone to get into heaven?" Take the opportunity to point out that salvation is by God's grace.

Prayer

Lord thank You that salvation is a gift from You. We cannot earn the gift by our efforts or by giving of our money. Help each member of our family to trust in You alone for salvation. Amen.

Day Four

Luther at the Door: Part 2

Scripture Reading: Romans 1:16-17

"I beat importunately upon Paul at Romans 1:17 most ardently desiring to know what Paul wanted" (Luther).

Not only did Luther knock on the church door he also knocked on the door of Paul's epistle to the Romans. *For in it [the gospel] the righteousness of God is revealed from heaven against all ungodliness and unrighteousness of men, who suppress the truth in unrighteousness..." (Romans 1:17).*

It was at this door where Luther first found clarity and comfort for his tormented soul. The problem for Luther centered on God's holiness and man's sinfulness. The Church taught that the saints of old had left a treasury of merit that could be drawn upon and distributed to the people through the purchase of indulgences. Indulgences symbolized both the errant theology of the Church and her corruption. That being the case— what was the answer?

From Luther's study of the Bible came his conviction that salvation is by grace through faith in Christ alone. We will seek to understand more fully later in this book some of the key theological points of Luther and the other Reformers.

Family Activity

The church door in Luther's Day was a place where community announcements and issues for debate were placed. Take a bulletin board and have your children place slips of paper with family announcements for the upcoming week as well as questions about the Bible and the Reformation. Later in the week schedule a time to discuss their questions. For younger children have them draw a picture of Luther nailing his 95 theses to the church door (you might show them a picture from the Internet of the Castle Church door in Luther's day).

Prayer

Lord we thank You for the glorious gospel of Christ. You alone can save sinners. Thank You for grace. Amen

Day Five

Boars and Bulls

Scripture Reading: Galatians 1:6-10

Did you know that Martin Luther was once referred to as a "wild boar" by the pope? Pope Leo sent an official document that contained these words, "Arise, O Lord and judge Thy cause. A wild boar has invaded Thy vineyard." It took several months before Luther received the document which condemned forty-one of his beliefs and called on him to repent or else face punishment. This document was a "papal bull." A papal bull was an authoritative document that bore the official seal of the pope.

Some sixty days after Luther received the papal bull he and some students burned it.

The pope sent the bull because Luther was challenging the theology of the Church. As we have discovered, Luther taught against indulgences. He also raised questions about the real authority of the pope. Luther argued that though the pope can err the Bible does not. He also taught that the only biblical sacraments of the church were baptism and the Lord's Supper. The major theological point for Luther was the doctrine of justification by faith. For Luther man could not be saved by any contribution of his own merits or the merits of any other saint dead or alive. Man cannot be saved by good works because he has a sin nature. Only by faith in Jesus Christ can a sinner be saved from their sins.

Luther would not compromise. He stood his ground and burned the bull. As a result Luther was excommunicated from the church and summoned to appear at the Diet of Worms. We will learn more about that Diet in the next chapter.

Family Activity

Make a copy of an official document. Write on the document; "Luther repent or else face punishment." If you have a fireplace, take the document and burn it. Your goal is to give your children a sense of the historical event. Luther was increasingly becoming an opponent of the teaching of the Roman church because he was discovering that they were preaching a different gospel than the one contained in the Bible.

Prayer

Lord we acknowledge that we need Your strength in order to stand strong when others challenge us because of our faith in Christ. Please help us to learn to increasingly rely on Your power for the challenges that we face. Help us to be discerning and to quickly recognize error when it comes our way. Amen.

Day Six

A Diet of Worms

Scripture Reading: Acts 14:1-7

Probably most of you are not accustomed to sitting down to a dinner of worms. Such a dinner would be a bit distasteful, to say the least.

Martin Luther was summoned to appear before the Diet of Worms in the spring of 1521. Diet means assembly. The assembly was made up of political and religious leaders as well as a few of Luther's friends. Worms is a small village in Germany.

This Diet would be a turning point in the Reformation. Luther faced the most powerful earthly authorities of his day. If he failed, the work of reform in Germany would be greatly hindered. If he stood strong he might lose his life and Luther's participation in the Reformation would end. God was not dependent upon Luther but He chose to use him to accomplish His great purposes. God always has a witness to His name. If He had chosen for Luther to have been murdered His work would have continued.

Luther was like David facing Goliath. The Church and the State stood against Luther. He would need courage to be faithful as he faced such giants.

Family Activity

Take a globe or atlas and help your children to find Germany and some of the key places in Germany that we have been discussing this month. A "Google" search of images of Wittenberg and Worms will give a picture of places that were instrumental in the Reformation. Take some time to pray for Germany that the gospel would again spread through the land. Get information about missionaries that you can pray for.

Prayer

Lord thank You for giving David the strength to overcome Goliath and thank You for enabling Martin Luther to stand against the false teaching of his day. You are strong. Please magnify Your strength in our family. Amen.

Day Seven

No Horns and No Teeth

Scripture Reading: Acts 5:17-32

The Reformation was a time in which the Bible was rediscovered, dusted off and made available to the common man. For many years the truth of Scripture had been concealed by church leaders. The Bible was hidden behind layers of tradition and was considered to be only one source of authority. The church did not want the common person to read the Bible for themselves. During Luther's day the Church believed that the pope and the church were primary sources of authority and that the Bible's authority was derived from the first two authorities.

When Luther stood before the assembly at the Diet of Worms he was asked to recant much of his teaching and writing. This was not an easy experience for Luther as he stood before the powerful Church and State. In fact Luther became fearful and asked for more time to consider and pray. The day after his request he appeared again before the assembly and was asked again to recant. Leaders of Church and State wanted Luther to reply "without horns and without teeth"—that is simply. Luther's response was faithful and heroic. He said, "Since Your Majesty and your lordships desire a simple reply, I will answer without horns and without teeth. Unless I am convicted by Scripture and plain reason I do not accept the authority of popes and councils, for they have contradicted each other—my conscience is captive to the Word of God, I cannot and I will not recant anything, for to go against conscience is neither right nor safe. God help me, Amen."

Luther was saying that the Word of God alone was the determiner of His convictions and His actions. The Scripture is to direct the life of a Christian. That being said the Bible recognizes certain authorities that God has ordained. He has ordained civil, family and church authorities. The faithful Christian must be submissive to those authorities unless they seek to bind his conscience in contradiction to the Bible. In that case the Christian must obey God by making sure that his "conscience is captive to the Word of God."

Luther stood on the Bible. What about you?

Luther left Worms but his life was in danger. The pope forbid him to preach, commanded that his writings be burned and the emperor said that Luther could be killed. On Luther's way back to Wittenberg he was kidnapped. However, he was kidnapped by friends and taken to the castle of Wartburg where he was protected for a year and then he returned home. Luther wrote constantly during that time and completed a German translation of the New Testament in 1522.

Luther died in 1546 after a fruitful life of ministry and he was buried at the church in Wittenberg. His legacy lives on. We are recipients of his commitment to the Bible.

Family Activity

Consider the acronym below as a help to developing your own. Create an acronym using words like; Luther, Calvin, Reformation and others. Acronyms are effective teaching tools.

R. Reclaiming the Truth *The Reformers held up Scripture as authoritative.*

E. Engaging in Preaching *The Reformation saw preaching restored to a central place.*

F. Fighting the Fight *Faithful Reformers fought the good fight of faith and many suffered and died as a result.*

O. Overturning Abuses *Abuses such as indulgences and theological error were prevalent in the church.*

R. Reading the Bible *The Reformers sought to put the Bible into the language of the people.*

M. Marriage Restored *The church forbid its leaders from marrying. Luther married a former nun.*

A. Affirming Theology *The Reformation was a theological movement where salvation by grace was affirmed.*

T. Teaching the Young *Education was emphasized by the Reformers. John Calvin's Geneva was called by John Knox as "the most perfect school of Christ on the earth since the days of the Apostles."*

I. Insisting on faith alone *Sola Fide, or faith alone, was a fundamental doctrine of the Reformation. Without this doctrine Luther said the church would fall.*

O. Onward from Germany *The Reformation spread from Germany to Switzerland to the Netherlands to England and to America.*

N. Narrowing the number of sacraments *The 16th century church had seven sacraments. Luther and the other Reformers believed that the Bible taught only two sacraments or ordinances—those being baptism and the Lord's Supper.*

Prayer

Lord thank You that You have given us the Bible which makes known to us Your character and will. Help us to grow in our understanding of Your truth that we might be strong in faith giving glory to You. Amen.

Day Eight

A Preacher and a Patriot: Part 1

Scripture Reading: Acts 20:17-37; Mark 9:38-41

The Reformation produced powerful ripples. It spread outward and touched many other countries. One of the ripples landed on the soil of Switzerland. Ulrich Zwingli was born in 1484 and like Luther had the benefits of a good education. He learned Greek, Hebrew and Latin which would be of great help to him in his later ministry. His father also saw to it that he knew and understood Swiss history. This, no doubt, was one of the reasons that Zwingli was such a patriot. Though he became a Catholic priest in 1506 he increasingly became convinced of Reformation doctrine. As a preacher in Zurich, crowds flocked to hear him. However, he was more than a preacher—Zwingli should be remembered as a faithful pastor. The plague came to Zurich killing more than two thousand people. Zwingli bravely took the risks that were associated with visiting those that were infected. Eventually he became infected and was sick for several months. He survived and along with him his example of faithful pastoral ministry.

Zwingli and Luther did not agree on everything. One of their most passionate debates was over the doctrine of The Lord's Supper. Zwingli desired to have fellowship with Luther though the two of them disagreed. However, Luther felt that they could not have unity. This is one of the sad accounts of the Reformation. Both Luther and Zwingli believed in the importance of the Lord's Supper. Their differences were significant. It seems that Luther was too hardened in his stance against Zwingli since they were in agreement on many other points. The result was a split creating the Reformed and Lutheran branches of the Protestant Church. Other rifts would come to the Reformation among men who had significant agreement but differed over some point of theology.

It is important that we do not compromise the truth. However, godly Christians will disagree on their understanding of certain elements of doctrine. The distinctions are important. However, Christians should humbly learn from one another and have discernment to know when and if they can have fellowship with one who has a different understanding of certain biblical doctrines.

Family Activity

Zwingli is remembered as a faithful preacher and Pastor. In our Scripture reading today Paul's ministry was recounted before the church elders. He charged them to be faithful pastors of the church. What are some of the qualities of your pastor? Write them down. Pray for him and send a note of appreciation for his ministry of caring for you by preaching God's Word.

Prayer

Lord thank You for the example of Zwingli who risked his life in order to minister to his suffering people. Thank You for our pastor and we pray that You would encourage him in his work. Help us to be willing to learn from those who differ from us without compromising our convictions. Help us to grow in our understanding of Scripture so that our convictions will be biblical.

Day Nine

A Preacher and a Patriot: Part 2

Scripture Reading: 2 Timothy 2:1-13

Zwingli's influence grew with his faithfulness to preach the Bible. The Reform Church was established in Switzerland and the country was divided between the Reformed and the Catholic. Military and theological battles broke out and the land was filled with much heartache. As you study the time of the Reformation you will discover that the church and state were much more closely aligned in that time than is the case today in most countries.

Zurich was invaded. Zwingli demonstrated that he was a preacher and a patriot. He served as a chaplain of the Army. Just as he had been a faithful Pastor during the plague, he tenderly cared for those that experienced the physical and mental scars of battle. Hundreds of the citizens of Zurich were killed in battle including Zwingli. Zwingli, while caring for a fallen solider, was seriously injured and then persecuted by the opposing army. Zwingli's body was cut up into pieces, burned and his ashes scattered. This, like many Reformation events, occurred in the month of October. The year was 1531. Zwingli was only forty-six or forty-seven years old. A statue of Zwingli stands in Zurich where he is portrayed with a Bible in one hand and a sword in the other. Zwingli was a preacher and a patriot.

Family Activity

Use your globe and find Switzerland and the city of Zurich. Consider its location in relationship to Germany and the United States. Remind your children that this is where Zwingli lived, preached and served as a chaplain in the army. This is also where he died as a preacher and a patriot. Pray for Switzerland that the gospel would spread through missionary activity and faithful churches

Prayer

Lord help us to cultivate hearts of compassion towards those that are sick, injured and needy. Please open many doors in Switzerland for the gospel to spread and call missionaries who will faithfully proclaim Your name. Amen.

Day Ten

The Fugitives: Part 1

Scripture Reading: Hebrews 11: 32-40

The television series, "The Fugitive" was popular when I was young. The show was based on a true story of a doctor accused of a crime that he claimed he did not commit—and in the show (at least) he was innocent of murdering his wife. He escaped from the authorities and spent his life on the run. A fugitive is a person on the run.

A group of Christians during the time of the Reformation were on the run from both Reformed and Catholic authorities. These people were derisively nicknamed the "Anabaptist." The prefix "ana" means "again." What lead to the nickname?

The key leaders of the Anabaptist movement had grown up in the Roman Catholic Church. Many of them had been in church leadership. Over time, through the study of Scripture and the influence of men like Martin Luther and Ulrich Zwingli, they embraced the Reformation and the doctrine of *sola scriptura*. Their study of Scripture opened up new thinking to these Anabaptists who have often been referred to as "radicals" and the leaders of the "radical Reformation."

Though the early Anabaptists had a number of things in common with the other Reformers they also had some major differences.

Some of their differences included a belief that baptism was only for believers and not for infants. The Anabaptists believed in a clear separation between church and state and most were pacifists (they did not believe in fighting in wars). They wanted a simple church and community that was based on the teachings of the New Testament.

Luther and Zwingli were committed to infant baptism and a strong union between church and state. They were greatly distraught over the development of the Anabaptist movement.

Still today Christian theologians and historians debate the pros and cons of the Anabaptist movement. Some find many positives from the Anabaptists. Others see primarily negatives. Whatever your position it is a fact that the Anabaptist movement had a significant impact on the Reformation.

Family Activity

Today is a good opportunity to have a family "pow-wow" session and discuss some important issues. The sentences below can serve to start your discussion. Of course this will primarily be for older children and teenagers but you should also take opportunity to teach your younger children how to get along with friends that they may disagree with.

What should Christians do when they disagree with one another? There are certain Biblical doctrines that all true Christians agree on. For example, all true Christians believe that Jesus is

God and that He lived a sinless life, died on the cross for sinners and was raised from the dead. However, many godly Christians have differing views on baptism, the relationship between the church and the state, matters of eschatology and the present ministry of the Holy Spirit. On those matters we may agree to disagree without compromising our convictions. Of course we should always be ready to change our beliefs as we grow in our understanding of the Bible. Distinctions are not unimportant. Such distinctions over issues like baptism lead Christians to unite with churches that are likeminded. However, though one might unite, for example, with a Baptist church and another with a Presbyterian church—there is often much common ground that can lead to fellowship between Christians who differ. Help your children to understand the essential doctrines of the Christian faith. Lead them to a biblical perspective as to why you attend the church that you do. An encouraging modern movement is Together for the Gospel (TFG). TFG is made up of Christian leaders who are unified in their understanding of the biblical gospel but who have differences in other important areas.

Prayer

Lord please grant to us discernment that we may know the truth and recognize error. Help us to learn from true Christians who differ from us and to unite with them around the gospel of Christ. Forgive us when we are uncharitable towards those with whom we have areas of disagreement. Amen.

Day Eleven

The Fugitives: Part 2

Scripture Reading: Matthew 28:16-20

In the 16th century there were laws requiring infant baptism. Therefore, in January of 1524 when Conrad Grebel baptized George Blaurock, a great controversy arose. Grebel, Blaurock and others had been meeting for Bible study in Blarouck's home in Zurich. This in itself had raised the eyebrows of city leaders. After Blaurock was baptized nearly 100 more people were baptized the next few weeks. All were baptized as adults and following their profession of faith in Jesus Christ. These Anabaptists believed that baptism was for believers only.

Grebel, Blaurock and another leader-- Felix Manz were summoned to the town council where they debated Zwingli. Zwingli was a far superior debater and therefore won the support of the City Council against the Anabaptists.

The Anabaptists were exiled from Zurich and became fugitives. They were persecuted by both by the Reformed and Catholic churches. Many were hunted down and martyred. One such leader was Michael Sattler who was burned at the stake on May 21, 1527. Several days later his wife was drowned.

A number of groups were (and are) representative of Anabaptist theology. One such group was led by Menno Simons. His followers were later known as the Mennonites.

Though a careful study of the Anabaptists would reveal much that we might disagree with, they nevertheless have left us an example that we can learn from.

They opposed hierarchical views of church leadership and structure and preferred to be called brethren. Let us learn from their humility. They also sought to establish their churches on the teaching of the New Testament. This they learned from the Bible and from the Reformers. Though we may disagree on some of their interpretations we should appreciate their commitment.

One of the sad stories of the Reformation is that Zwingli consented to the persecution of the Anabaptists. He assumed that he was doing right by punishing those he considered heretics. Zwingli participated in the death of the Anabaptist leader, Felix Manz. Manz was in and out of prison and threatened time and again for his advocacy of Anabaptist theology. He continued to evangelize and baptize. Finally, with the consent of Zwingli he was bound and drowned. He died singing a prayer of commitment of his spirit into the hands of God.

History does not smile on Zwingli for his persecution of the Anabaptists. Zwingli was a great man in many respects but he erred on this point.

Not all of the Anabaptists were godly men. Some were extremely radical in their views and practices. Some were, no doubt, heretics. However, we should not let the bad examples cause us to lose the positive lessons of those who were courageous Reformers. They stood for what they believed and were willing to suffer the consequences for it. There may be a time when we find ourselves on the run from those who would seek to prohibit us from worshiping God as our conscience dictates. Our faith may be tested in ways that lead to our death. And even if we are never forced to die for our convictions let us pray that God would give us courage to daily stand for His truth.

Family Activity

Profiles in Courage is a memorable book by John F. Kennedy. If you have a copy of that book, show it to your children. The Reformation is filled with profiles in courage. Men and women considered it a privilege to be allowed to suffer for Christ. Visit the web-site www.persecution.com and read with your children the accounts of some modern day people who are indeed a profile in courage.

Prayer

Lord thank You for the example of faithful men and women who willingly suffered for the sake of the gospel. If we are called upon to suffer help us to not deny our faith. Amen.

Day Twelve

A Man Named John: Part 1

Scripture Reading: Psalm 37:23; Proverbs 16:9

Gerard Calvin dreamed of a bright future for his son John. His plan was that John would become a priest. Due to a dispute with a church leader, Gerard changed his mind about young John's future. John would study law. John developed a sharp mind and became a good writer. He was influenced by the teaching of Martin Luther, therefore recognizing the errors of the established church.

We might refer to John as a bookworm because he loved to read and study. However, his study was fueled by love for God. He wanted to know God and to live his life in accordance with the Bible.

Because of John's increasingly Protestant position he faced the threat of persecution and had to move from Paris to the city of Basel. Calvin escaped from Paris out of a back window while his friends detained the authorities who came to arrest him. The next day Calvin left for Basel disguised as a farmer. While in Basel he helped with a translation of the Bible into the French language. He began writing *The Institutes of the Christian Religion*. This would become one of the most important works in the history of the Christian church.

Gerard Calvin had a plan for his son John and he set out to see that John followed the plan. John was obedient to the instruction of his father. The Lord directed John's steps leading him from Paris to Basel where Calvin began to make investments in writing that continues to impact the Christian world. Calvin himself would say, "My father had intended me for theology from my early childhood...then changing his mind, he set me to learning law...until God at last turned my course in another direction by the secret rein of his providence." *(Sketches from Church History* S.M. Houghton).

Family Activity

Sketch out a map from your house to a local business or school. Chart on the map the course that you would normally take. Then imagine that the road is closed due to a car wreck or storm. What alternate route would you take to get to your desired location? What plans have you made for your family that have not come to pass? Perhaps you can remember a time when plans were completely changed and your life was redirected. Help your family to understand that God is trustworthy and even when we make bad decisions that He is still directing our paths. Look on the globe to check the location of France in relationship to Germany, Switzerland and the United States.

Prayer

Lord help us to make wise decisions with confidence that You will direct our steps. Thank You for redirecting the life of John Calvin and for blessing us as a result. Amen.

Day Thirteen

A Man Named John: Part 2

Scripture Reading: 2 Corinthians 5:1-11

The Reformation provided a rich example of hard work. From Luther to Calvin and later the Puritans, diligence in one's work was a mark of a godly person who sought to do all things to God's glory.

John Calvin could never be rightly accused of laziness. His theology of work grew out of his conviction that he was accountable to God. Therefore when Calvin moved to Basel he labored with diligence. The first edition of Calvin's *Institutes of the Christian Religion* was published in Basel. Pen and paper wedded to a brilliant and God-fearing mind is a powerful instrument. Such is the case with Calvin and *The Institutes*.

Eventually, John left Basel. His plan was to settle down in the city of Strasbourg. In God's providence he traveled through Geneva, Switzerland where he would spend the night. A passionate preacher named William Farel lived in Geneva.

Farel visited Calvin during his overnight visit. He believed that God wanted John to stay in Geneva and help cultivate the progress of the Reformation. Farel believed that God might judge Calvin if he did not remain in Geneva and labor for reform. Calvin feared God and decided to remain, but as much as possible, to keep to a life of quiet study and devotion. It is important for us to note that John was only 27 years old.

John's work in Geneva is still studied today. His ministry was one of teaching, writing and seeking to help the people regulate their lives according to the Scripture. However, his ministry in Geneva would face some great challenges that would threaten the work of the Reformation. His work would not be quiet and he would feel the persecution that comes to those who serve Jesus.

Family Activity

Take a Bible concordance and look up passages related to working hard, being diligent and living a disciplined life. Have each member of your family read aloud a verse. Draw a picture of a target. What did Paul make as his goal (2 Corinthians 5:9)? Write Paul's aim in the center of the target. One of the teachings recovered during the Reformation was "calling" or "vocation". In the years prior to the Reformation, "calling" was reserved for church work only. The Reformers believed that the Bible taught that all of life is for God's glory and therefore the butcher, merchant or housewife were all called of God into His service. The Reformers had a sacred view of work.

Prayer

Lord You are the creator of work. Therefore, we recognize work as one way that we can glorify You. Help us to be fruitful and joyful in the work that You have given us as a family and to try to make a positive difference in the lives of others. Amen.

Day Fourteen

A Man Named John: Part 3

Scripture Reading: 2 Timothy 4:1-5

John Calvin and William Farel were co-laborers in the gospel. However their disciplined ministry put them in disfavor with some leaders in Geneva. This led to John and William being exiled. To be exiled means to be sent away from one's home, city or country.

John went to Strasbourg where he became a preacher to French refugees. There he would carry on the work of reformation that he had begun in Geneva. Advancing the Reformation meant reforming the worship of the church, educating the people and cultivating a perspective of the Lordship of Jesus over all things.

God would bless his ministry in Strasbourg and would bring a godly woman into his life, a widow named Idelette. John's marriage to Idelette de Bure would bring him both joy and suffering. She was a wonderful wife for John and was of great assistance to him in his ministry. Calvin called Idelette "the excellent companion of his life." Idelette gave birth to, what would be John's only child, a son. The son lived only about a week.

Idelette lived only a few years more. John's heart was grieved, but his theology of a sovereign and righteous God encouraged him.

John was a faithful minister in Strasbourg. There he had much time and freedom to write. In Geneva the work of reform was in great danger due to the threat of the Roman Church. Eventually, it was determined by city leaders to bring Calvin back to Geneva to continue the work that he had begun several years earlier. John was hesitant to return because of the great persecution that he had faced there, but finally determined that God wanted Him back in Geneva. His pulpit ministry at Geneva had been focused on teaching God's word verse by verse. When he returned to the church in Geneva in 1541 he picked up where he had left off three years earlier. Such was John's commitment to preaching the Bible which was foundational to the work of reform in the church and city.

Family Activity

One of the contributions of the Reformation was the recovery of marriage as a good gift from God. The Roman Church forced its leaders to remain unmarried. The Puritans considered such coercion as ungodly. They based their analysis on I Timothy 4:1-4. The Puritans wrote extensively on the joy of a Christian marriage and family. God provided Katie for Luther and Idelette for Calvin. A godly spouse is a great blessing from God. However, marriage brings with it many difficulties. John and Idelette would suffer the pains of having a child die. Idelette had already lost one husband to death and she would live only a few years after her marriage to John. Children thank God for your parent(s). Pray for a family that you know who is suffering.

Here are some Reformation era quotes on marriage:

> "Let the wife make the husband glad to come home, and let him make her sorry to see him leave." (Martin Luther)

> "The man whose heart is endeared to the woman he loves...dreams of her in the night, hath her in his eye and apprehension when he awakes, museth on her as he sits at the table, walks with her when he travels...She lies in his bosom, and his heart trusts in her, which forceth all to confess that the stream of his affection, like a mighty current, runs with full tide and strength." (Thomas Hooker)

Prayer

Lord thank You for biblical teaching about marriage and the family that was recovered during the Reformation. Thank You for providing Katie for Luther and Idelette for Calvin. Help our family to grow in godliness and to be enabled to suffer for Your sake.

Day Fifteen

A Man Named John: Part 4

Scripture Reading: Revelation 1:9; 22:14-21

Christians have often referred to God's kingdom on earth as a "shining city on a hill." Under John Calvin's ministry Geneva was such a city. This became more evident during his second term of ministry in Geneva. Calvin's theology led the people to embrace a worldview of God's control over all of life. Calvin's teaching lead to a thorough educational system in Geneva. You need to remember that Calvin taught the Bible throughout the week and on Sunday. He wrote commentaries on most books of the Bible. His shorter writings were widely distributed in his lifetime via tracts and booklets. He was tireless in his efforts to teach and reform. The atmosphere in Geneva was filled with the aroma of Calvin's faithful teaching. Geneva became a place where persecuted Christians from other areas of the world could find refuge from difficulty. Young people as well as ministers of the gospel were trained in Calvin's Geneva. It was in Geneva that Puritan refugees developed the great "Geneva Bible" which became the Bible most used by the Puritans and other Reformation minded Christians in Europe.

As John grew older he became increasingly frail but he continued to work. He knew the pains of suffering attacks from his opponents, even as his body grew increasingly weak. He soldiered on. He did not want to fail to be faithful to God. In a period of suffering he said, *"Would you that the Lord should find me idle when He comes?"* He died on May 27, 1564 at age 54. No one knows the exact location of his grave site- and that is the way that he would have wanted it. Though we remember John Calvin as one of the great heroes in Christian history his desire was that God would be glorified through his life and ministry. He was not a perfect man. He had some glaring weaknesses. However, John was a faithful man and his influence is still felt the world over.

Family Activity

A worldview is simply a way of looking at the world. Draw a picture of eye glasses. Write across the lens the word "God." A worldview is like putting on a pair of glasses that remind us to view the world through the lens of God's glory and God's will.

Prayer

Lord help us to think first about God's glory as we view our world. Help us to daily look through Your eyes as we consider what to believe and how to live. Thank You for giving us Your word that directs our steps. Amen.

Day Sixteen

Lessons from Calvin

Scripture Reading: Hebrews 13:7

John Calvin would have been content with the quiet life of a scholar. He did not envision himself to be on the front-lines of the Reformation as it spread across Europe. However, God used him as perhaps the most important human figure in the practical work of the Reformation.

Some of the lessons that we can learn from Calvin:

1. **Study**. The faithful Christian should be a diligent student of the Bible.
2. **Regulate**. The godly person and faithful congregation should always be seeking to regulate their lives by the teaching of the Bible.
3. **Discipline**. Much is lost in life due to a lack of discipline. Often the difference between a great and a mediocre life is discipline. The disciplined life requires a willingness to "endure hardship as a good solider of Jesus Christ" (2 Timothy 2).
4. **Sensitivity**. John Calvin was sensitive to the Spirit of God. That is one of the reasons that

he followed Farel's counsel to help in the ministry at Geneva.

5. **Faithfulness.** As John neared death some of his friends (understandably) wanted him to slow down and rest. John wanted to make sure that he finished his life in a manner well pleasing to God. He was faithful to the end.

6. **God's glory.** John Calvin was driven by a passion for God's glory. He would have, no doubt, been uncomfortable with the sort of attention that we give him today. His great desire was that God would be glorified in all things.

These are lessons that we should teach our children by example and through instruction. Though we want our children to have times of play we also want them to learn to study and regulate their lives in accordance with the Bible. We want them to learn to discipline themselves and to be sensitive to the Holy Spirit. We should desire that our children learn to be faithful in small things so that they will be faithful in larger matters. Teach your children these things.

Family Activity

Countless people have been influenced by the ministry of Calvin and his work at Geneva. One couple that was profoundly influenced by Calvin was Francis and Edith Schaeffer. Do a search to uncover a sketch of their ministry in Switzerland.

Consider purchasing a copy of the book *L'Abri* that tells the story of the Schaeffer's ministry.

C. Confront the culture with the truth. *Calvin was a preacher of the Word.*
A. Acquire knowledge and wisdom from study. *Calvin was a student.*
L. Live a faithful life. *Calvin was diligent in his duties.*
V. Voice a vision for God's glory. *Calvin had a vision for God's glory.*
I. Invest in the lives of others. *Calvin established educational opportunities for all.*
N. Never resort to laziness. *Calvin feared being lazy because he wanted to please God.*

Prayer

Lord we pray for Your help as we seek to study Your word, discipline ourselves to be godly, regulate our lives according to Scripture, to be sensitive to Your Spirit, faithful in Your work and to live our lives according to Your glory. Amen

Day Seventeen

Lessons from Geneva

Scripture Reading: Luke 2:52;
I Timothy 3:15-16; 2 Timothy 2:15

Though Christians often debate the relationship between church and state we nonetheless can learn a lot about church ministry from Calvin's Geneva.

1. The Church is to be a place of **restoration**. Geneva became a place of refuge and protection for many of God's servants who fled there in the midst of persecution. Local churches should have open doors and provide rest, nourishment and relief for fellow Christians who suffer.
2. The Church is to be a place that encourages **education**. Calvin led the church and city to work towards educational reform. Young children learned by means of catechism. Older children studied the Scripture, the classics, Latin, logic, history and rhetoric. Though the primary function of the Pastor is preaching the word, he should, nonetheless, be promoting growth in all of life. Studying the Reformers reminds us that all truth is God's truth. That does not mean that all truth is equal to Bible truth. The Bible is unique as

it is the inerrant revelation from God to man. Education is to be focused on improving God-given resources for His glory.

3. The church is to be a place of **proclamation**. Geneva was divided up into Parishes and ministers were assigned teaching and pastoral duties in those Parishes. The primary function of the preacher was to preach. Calvin often preached at least once a day and sometimes more.

The Scottish Reformer, John Knox, called Geneva "the most perfect school of Christ on the earth."

Family Activity

The Bible tells us that Jesus grew physically, spiritually, intellectually and socially. That is the model that Geneva was built upon under the leadership of Calvin. The church stood on and held up the truth that the entire community was to be a place where diligence was promoted. With your children write out examples of how your church and community can better reflect biblical principles.

Geneva was characterized by: RESTORATION: EDUCATION: PROCLAMATION

Prayer

Lord help our family, church and community to be places where people are restored and trained and help our church to be faithful to preach the Word. Amen.

Day Eighteen

A Sickly King and a Bloody Queen

Scripture Reading: 2 Corinthians 12:9-10;
1 Timothy 2:1-6; Hebrews 11:36-40

King Henry VIII is well known for his many wives. However, as a devout Roman Catholic, he was also something of a theologian. He even put his theological musings into writing when he published a defense of the Roman Catholic Church. As a result of his defense of Catholicism he was given the title of "Defender of the Faith" by the pope. It might properly be said, though, that Henry's greatest commitment was not to the Roman Church but to himself.

Henry was married to Catherine but she was unable to provide him with a son. Therefore he wanted his marriage annulled (rendered void by the church). The pope would not grant the annulment and therefore Henry broke ties with the pope and decided to set himself up as the head of the church. He did not need the pope's permission to do what he wanted to do.

He made Thomas Cranmer archbishop and had him annul the marriage. Henry then married a woman by the name of Anne Boleyn whom he later executed to marry Jane Seymour. Jane gave birth to Edward. Henry had his son.

When Henry died, Edward became the King of England at age nine or ten. Edward was sickly and only lived until age 16. However, Edward was a godly man and had biblically minded men around him. The Reformation in England advanced under his leadership. When Edward was inaugurated he insisted on a Bible being carried into the ceremony. He wanted everyone to know of his commitment to the Scripture. Edward, though young, was very wise. He knew four languages and especially loved to read the Bible. He had also been privileged to hear John Knox and other godly men preach.

Many of the trappings of Roman Catholicism were removed under Edward's leadership and new articles of faith were established. Edward had the Bible distributed throughout the land and he established multiple ministries of mercy to help needy people. Edward was a bright light in the English Reformation. Some of his last words recorded in *Foxe's Book of Martyrs* are a prayer, "O my Lord God, defend this realm from papistry, and maintain the true religion, that I and my people may praise Thy holy name..."

When Edward died on July 6, 1553, it seemed like the Reformation in England died with him. With the ascendancy of Mary to the throne, dark days followed for those who held to Reformation theology.

Mary is remembered as "Bloody Mary" because, in her passion to rid England of anything Protestant, she was willing to murder Christian leaders. Though Mary's ascendancy delayed the fruit of Edward's reforms, God's work marched forward. The blood of the martyrs indeed would flow through those who followed their example of courage and faithfulness in preaching the true gospel. During the reign of Bloody

Mary the church had a faithful writer by the name of John Foxe.

Foxe wrote in intricate detail of the death of many faithful men and women during Mary's reign of terror. Since its publication it has been common to find Foxe's *Book of Martyrs* in the homes of Christians. That book has served to strengthen and comfort Christians who have faced the struggles of suffering.

God used Edward to plant seeds of reform in English soil. Those seeds would grow after the bloody reign of Mary. Though the reformation progress may have slowed down under Mary, we can give glory to God that he used a sickly king to advance the Reformation. Though Edward was not physically strong we can readily see God's glory during Edward's reign from 1547-1553.

Family Activity

Use a whiteboard to draw the family tree of King Henry. Who were some of the biblically minded men that surrounded Edward? Discuss how God uses human frailties in such a way that He is glorified. You might consider a study that would enable you to list some of the reforms that God used Edward to bring to England.

Prayer

Lord thank You that You are not dependent on the physical health of Your servants to accomplish Your purposes. Help us to see Your glory in how You used a sickly King to accomplish Your purposes. Thank You for the faithful men and women who suffered and died because of their love for You. Help us to remember and to follow their faith. Amen.

Day Nineteen

Lighting a Candle

Scripture Reading: Acts 6:8-15, 7:55-60,
Revelation 2:13

William Tyndale had a key passion in life and that was to put the Bible into the language and hands of the common man. The Roman Catholic Church was opposed to the Bible being readily available. They forbade people to buy, sell, distribute or read the Bible. They even purchased and burned many of Tyndale's New Testaments. Tyndale's work of Bible translation led him to be persecuted. He was eventually betrayed into the hands of the authorities, imprisoned and later tried and condemned as a heretic. On October 6, 1536 after a year and a half in prison he was tied to the stake, strangled and burned. His last words were, "Lord, open the King of England's eyes." In God's providence Tyndale's work was gathered up and along with the work of a man by the name of Miles Coverdale the entire Bible was made available in English. After several revisions it was called *The Great Bible* which was published in 1539. Amazingly King Henry ordered that a copy of that Bible be placed in every church in England. All of this is important to remember as you think of the events that transpired after Henry's death.

Under King Edward and his bishop Thomas Cranmer the Reformation advanced in England. However, the advancement was short-lived. Edward died in 1553 and Henry's daughter Mary was next in line for the throne. A group of leaders attempted an ill-fated attempt to put the Protestant Lady Jane Grey upon the throne. Her reign was short lived (nine days), as her small band of supporters was no match for the supporters of English tradition. Jane was removed from the throne and sent to The Tower of London. "Bloody Mary" extended mercy to young Jane offering her release in exchange for taking the Mass. Jane was a theologically astute woman of deep and courageous conviction. She refused to take the Mass and was martyred for her faith.

Jane represents the sort of character that the godly Reformers had. They were not perfect and sometimes faltered and erred, but they were noted for their courage.

Under the reign of "Bloody Mary," a number of Protestants were martyred including two bishops, Hugh Latimer and Nicholas Ridley. Latimer and Ridley were burned at the stake in 1555. As Ridley feared the fire, his friend Latimer uttered these now famous words, "Be of good comfort, Mr. Ridley, and play the man. We shall this day light a candle by God's grace, in England, as I trust shall never be put out."

The teaching, writing, and courageous example of many of the Reformers indeed lit a candle that burns brightly still today.

How can you light such a candle?

> *Read, study, learn, and love the Bible.*
> *Trust only in Christ for salvation.*
> *Seek God for the courage of your convictions.*
> *Invest your life in promoting God-centered reform.*

Family Activity

Light a candle. Feel the heat. Discuss ways people were martyred during the Reformation. Christians are still being martyred for their faith. Get a copy of Foxe's *Book of Martyrs* and read selections to your children. Thank God for the devotion and suffering of faithful servants of God. It is hard to believe now that there was a time when church leaders did not want people to read the Bible. Thank God for the freedom to own and read the Bible.

Prayer

Lord help our family to make a difference in the world in which we live in such a way that brings glory to You and impacts future generations. Amen.

Day Twenty

The Puritans: Part 1

Scripture Reading: Revelation 2:18-29

As the name suggests the Puritans were those who were interested in purifying the Church of England. The Puritans under Queen Elizabeth believed that the reforms begun by King Edward, halted by bloody Mary, but tolerated by Elizabeth (to some extent) were not enough. In their estimation the church had too much of the baggage of Rome, including even the clothing worn by ministers in their official duties. The Puritans believed that the Bible should regulate all of the affairs of the church. Most of the Puritans chose to remain and work for reform within the Church of England during Elizabeth's reign. However, Elizabeth did not like being challenged and she proved to be no friend to Puritanism and was more sympathetic to Catholicism. She did not want anyone criticizing the Church of England. Puritans would suffer much under Elizabeth. Some of the Puritans could no longer associate with the Church of England and they separated, thus earning the name Separatists. Elizabeth died in 1603 and James I became the King of England.

Those early Puritans are a reminder to us that we should constantly be seeking the purification of the church from beliefs and practices that are not biblical.

Reformation theology was grounded upon the belief that the Scripture is the sole rule of faith and practice for the church. The early Puritans did not want to separate from the English church but instead sought reform from within the church.

Though there are certainly situations that would lead a person to separate from a local church or denomination, perhaps the example of the Puritans would encourage one to first see if reform is possible before resorting to separation. The Separatists remind us that there indeed may be a time when a local church or denomination is so corrupt that reform is unlikely and to remain within the institution would lead to a compromise of convictions. The answers to such questions are often not simple. Let us seek wisdom from God.

Family Activity

Take a copy of your church bulletin and go through the order of worship and describe how the practices of your church are based in Scripture. If you find that the worship service of the church does not reflect a proper attention to prayer, Scripture reading, singing and preaching then pray for your church. Schedule a meeting with your pastor to humbly discuss the worship of the church. He may be able to give you some insight as to why the order of service printed in the church bulletin is structured as it is.

Prayer

Lord help our church to be increasingly reformed according to the Bible. Teach us to read, sing, pray and preach the Scripture more faithfully. Amen.

Day Twenty One

The Puritans: Part 2

Scripture Reading: 2 Timothy 3:16-17

When James I came to the throne of England, he was met with requests offered by hundreds of ministers. The ministers wanted James to consider further reforms for the church. Their aim was to rid the church of the trappings of Rome and to see established a more biblical church. The king in 1604 called a conference to deal with the ministers' petition. The result was not good for the Puritans. The king would make no real concessions to the requests and at least 300 ministers were deprived of their income. During the Reformation many Christian leaders lost earthly possessions, some lost their churches, others were stripped of their educational degrees, some were imprisoned and thousands were martyred.

A new translation of the Bible did come from the conference. The translation is the Authorized Version or "The King James Version." The new version was published in 1611. It was (and is) widely accepted and considered to be an accurate translation of the Bible.

King James was no true friend to the Puritans. Nevertheless, the sovereignty and the providence of God are evident in the events that transpired at the conference. As a result of the meetings this new translation of the Bible was widely distributed and no other translation of the Bible has had such a wide influence as the King James Version.

Family Activity

The sovereignty of God refers to His ownership and control of all things. God both lifts up and puts down kings and He does so for His own purposes. The sovereignty of God is comforting as we realize that God is righteous and good. Discuss the implications of God's sovereignty.

What can you learn about Bible translations? There are a number of good ones including the New American Standard Version, The English Standard Version, the New King James Version and The King James Version. Get a copy of a King James Version of the Bible and read the introductory remarks from King James to get a context for his part in the Reformation.

Prayer

Lord, You are a sovereign God. Though Christians are persecuted we acknowledge that You are working for the good of Your people in the midst of their suffering. Thank You for allowing us to have good translations of the Bible from which we can learn of Your sovereignty, righteousness, goodness and plan of salvation. Amen.

Day Twenty Two

The Puritans: Part 3

*Scripture Reading: Acts 13:1-5,14,51;
14:19-21; 15:30-35*

In spite of the set-backs and sufferings of the Puritans, their influence continued to grow and took root even among many governmental leaders. King Charles I followed James to the throne. He was married to a Roman Catholic and the seeds of discontent between the king and the increasingly Puritan parliament were sown. For eleven years, the king acted as a sort of dictator by ignoring Parliament. Many Puritan pastors were persecuted under Charles. Ultimately, a civil war between the followers of the king and the followers of Parliament erupted. Parliament was on the side of the Reformation and desired to summarize Reformation theology in a common confessional standard.

The result was a meeting of Puritan ministers at Westminster Abbey in London. There, some of the most influential documents in Christian history were written, including the *Westminster Confession of Faith.* These documents have had a profound influence on not only Presbyterians and Anglicans but other Reformation minded Christians such as

Reformed, Calvinistic Baptists. Baptists relied heavily on the *Westminster Confession of Faith* for their *1689 London Baptist Confession.*

As a result of the war, Puritanism became prominent in England and Scotland. Oliver Cromwell was the leader of the new Commonwealth. Many good things came from Cromwell and the Commonwealth but it was not an ideal state. When he died the Puritan Commonwealth died also and with the ascent of Charles II to the throne Puritan ministers would face once again great persecution.

Family Activity

Locate Scotland in comparison to the other countries of the Reformation and notice the gradual spread of the Reformation over the globe. Pray for a spiritual awakening and revival in England and Scotland. Pass around a copy of the *Westminster Confession of Faith* for your children to see.

Prayer

Lord thank You for confessions of faith and catechisms that faithfully communicate Your truth. Help us to hold to the faith when defending our convictions and in protecting our family from error. Amen.

Day Twenty Three

A Baptist named John

Scripture Reading: Acts 4:13-31

A faithful Christian and pastor who suffered greatly was a Baptist by the name of John Bunyan. John Bunyan is beloved still today primarily because of his great allegory, *The Pilgrim's Progress*. It has often been stated that this book is second only to the Bible in Christian influence. It is the story of the conversion of a man who lived in the City of Destruction. He flees the old city and begins a journey to the Celestial City. Along the way he meets both friends and enemies. The imagery that Bunyan paints in *Pilgrim's Progress* is vivid and instructive concerning the Christian journey. If you could only have one other book along with the Bible then *Pilgrim's Progress* would be an excellent selection. John Bunyan authored over 60 books, many of which are available still today.

Many know this John the Baptist because of *Pilgrim's Progress* but perhaps few know that he was not formally educated. He possessed great spiritual power in his preaching. The brilliant scholar John Owen intimated that he would gladly give up all of his knowledge if he could but have the power of Bunyan when preaching.

Bunyan suffered as a result of the acts of Charles II. Under his reign the clergy were required to submit to the *Book of Common Prayer*. Two thousand ministers refused to do so and that resulted in them losing their income and many were driven from their churches.

John Bunyan was not a member or leader in the Church of England and he was forbidden to preach. But like the godly before him he could not abide by a law that required him to forsake God's calling on his life. He was offered the opportunity to avoid prison if he would promise not to preach. You should know that John had a family that needed him including a blind daughter and a young wife. His heart, no doubt, felt the pains of being separated from his loved ones. However, John proved that he loved the Lord more than even his beloved family and chose to suffer affliction rather than violate his conscience.

Even in prison Bunyan remained a faithful pastor to his people through writing and by their visits. With pen and paper he did much good though locked behind prison bars. We should thank God that he used the simple Baptist named John to give us some of the most wonderful literature of the Puritan era.

Family Activity

Get an illustrated copy of *The Pilgrim's Progress* and commit to reading it at breakfast or another family gathering. Your children will enjoy the great illustrations found in many editions and the story will grab their attention. One of the best abridged children's editions is *The Dangerous Journey* (see the bibliography at the end of this book).

Prayer

Lord thank You for the great writings that were penned during the Puritan era. Thank You that many of those are still available to us today. As we read help us to learn more about the journey from conversion to heaven. Amen.

Day Twenty Four

Puritan Influence

Scripture Reading: Hebrews 12:1-4

The purpose and scope of this book does not allow for a detailed treatment of the Reformation. As it relates to the Puritans there are many leaders that you should know including William Perkins, Richard Sibbes, Thomas Goodwin, John Owen, Richard Baxter, Samuel Rutherford, Thomas Watson, Steven Charnock, Thomas Carlyle and John Bunyan, to name a very few. However, many later Christian leaders have also been referred to as Puritans because they held to the doctrines, practices and vision of the Puritans. Some of those later Puritans include men like George Whitfield, Jonathan Edwards and Charles Spurgeon. There are many such men and women (like Anne Bradstreet, the Puritan poet) that you and your children have opportunity to get to know. There are a variety of good biographies for children and adults available that will help you in your journey to discover these faithful Christians. We love these men and women because they point us upward to a great and holy God. We see His great work in their lives. Whether we recognize it or not we stand on the shoulders of the Reformers. Let us give due honor to those that have run the race before us as we keep our eyes on Christ.

The Puritans are often much maligned by those who do not know them very well or who choose to focus on their weaknesses. Perhaps you have heard people make fun of the Puritans. Like Luther, Zwingli, and Calvin the Puritans were fallen men, making mistakes but seeking to live for God's glory. It has often been said that it is difficult to estimate the size of a tree until it falls down. That is true of the Puritans. As thoughtful people have studied the Puritans they have discovered that they were giants of the faith and much of their teaching and living is worthy of imitation. In the past 25 years there has been a plethora of good Puritan books that has been republished. There have also been a number of wonderful books about the Puritans that have been written. An outstanding book about the Puritans is *A Quest for Godliness* by J.I. Packer. Consider purchasing a copy of this book and plan to dig deep into the lives and theology of the Puritans.

Family Activity

Find pictures in books or on the Internet of some of the Puritans. Tonight would be a fun time to dress in Puritan attire with your children. Have your children read aloud selections from *The Pilgrims Progress*.

Prayer

Lord we acknowledge that we are distracted by many things. Help us value learning through reading biographies of our Christian forefathers. Give us discernment as we seek to imitate their faithfulness and avoid their failures.

PART TWO

Catechism

Day Twenty Five

No Creed but Christ

Scripture Reading: Psalm 78:1-7

Christians have often recited the mantra, "no creed but Christ." The intent of such a statement may be well motivated, but the reality is that a creed, confession or catechism is simply a means of communicating biblical truth. Christians throughout history have recognized the need to clarify their understanding of Scripture, to summarize key doctrines in the face of error and to find ways of communicating the faith to their children. It has often been stated that one of the most effective ways of cultivating a biblical and theological reformation is in training children in the truths of the Christian faith. The usage of catechisms is one tool that many parents have used to train their children to learn the doctrines of the Bible. In using a catechism a parent will call out a question and await a response from their student. Historically, catechisms have been used in the church, the school and in the home. The Reformation has been called the golden age of catechisms and confessions.

Certainly all of these man-made documents must be measured by Scripture to see if they are helpful. The Reformation-era catechisms have stood the test of time and the scrutiny of faithful Bible students. They are helpful in passing the faith onward to future generations. As you use catechisms and confessions of faith make sure that you are clear that the Bible is the authority and the catechism or confession is merely a tool.

Get to know some of the key documents of the Reformation such as: The Belgic Confession (1561), The Heidelberg Catechism (1563) and The Canons of Dordt (1610). These three are often referred to as the "Three Forms of Unity." Even later statements such as the Westminster Confession of Faith (1646), the First (1644) and Second (1689) London Baptist Confessions of Faith all carry with them the smell of the Reformation and are built upon a solid Reformation foundation.

Family Activity

Survey a variety of catechisms and discuss the differences in their teachings. Make a commitment to commit one to memory and introduce a new question every week on a family bulletin board. A family favorite of ours is the Heidelberg Catechism which will be discussed in tomorrow's lesson.

Prayer

Lord we desire to learn more of Your word. Help us to utilize tools that honor You in helping us to commit Your truth to our hearts. Amen.

Day Twenty Six

Comfort

Scripture Reading: Romans 14:7-8

Life is difficult. You were already aware of that. However, do you know true comfort?

What is your only comfort in life and death?

In 1563, one of the most treasured writings in the history of the Christian church was published. The Heidelberg Catechism is one of the enduring documents from the time of the Reformation. It was well received in its time and is still loved today because of its theme of comfort.

Our world is fallen, a fact evident in everything from fading paint to heart disease, from broken marriages to the devastation of war. It is not simply the big events of life that challenge our comfort. It is also the daily decisions about diet and school, leaky roofs and overgrown lawns.

The Heidelberg Catechism reminds us of the only hope and comfort that is substantive and lasting. Recently I read of a funeral service for a five-year old little girl that included the first question and answer to the Heidelberg Catechism. Read the words and you will understand why the catechism would be appropriate when a loved one dies.

The first question of the Heidelberg Catechism:

"What is your only comfort in life and death?"

The answer is:

"That I, with body and soul, both in life and death, am not my own, but belong to my faithful Savior Jesus Christ; who with His precious blood has fully satisfied for all my sins, and delivered me from all the power of the devil; and so preserves me that without the will of my heavenly Father not a hair can fall from my head; yea, that all things must be subservient to my salvation, wherefore by His Holy Spirit He also assures me of eternal life, and makes me heartily willing and ready, henceforth to live unto Him."

Those are beautiful words.

Can you give the answer to the question of comfort with those same words? Do you know Jesus Christ like that?

Family Activity

Review the first question and answer to the Heidelberg Catechism. Break it down into parts and look for biblical passages that are reflected in the first answer. Discuss the theme of comfort with your children.

Prayer

Lord, You know that life is hard. The evidence of sin is everywhere. It is easy for us to grow discouraged in the midst of so many difficulties. Help us to anchor our lives to the comfort that You provide in Your word. Amen.

Day Twenty Seven

The Pathway to Comfort

Scripture Reading: I Corinthians 6:19-20

As we have learned, the Reformation brought to the church a number of confessions and catechisms. The Heidelberg Catechism was published in 1563 in Heidelberg, Germany. It was written to be used in both churches and schools. A catechism is a way to teach biblical truth by means of questions and answers. A question is asked and an answer is given regarding some point of the Christian faith. The Heidelberg Catechism speaks of a real, substantive, God-centered comfort.

The answer to the second question of the catechism gives the pathway to comfort.

"How many things are necessary for you to know, that you in this comfort may live and die happily?"

The answer:

"Three; the first, how great my sins and misery are; the second, how I am delivered from all my sins and misery; the third, how I am to be thankful to God for such deliverance."

Lasting comfort comes to those who understand the depth of their sinfulness, who know how to be delivered from their sins and misery and how to be thankful to God for such deliverance.

The catechism goes on to explain that though we are wicked sinners, Jesus is a great and glorious Savior. We are totally dependent upon a gracious God to grant deliverance to us from our sins and misery. We receive His gift by faith in His Son Jesus Christ. We then spend the rest of our lives learning from His Word how to be thankful to God for such a gift.

Do you know such deep and substantive comfort?

G.I. Williamson wrote a helpful volume that opens the door to catechisms in general and to the Heidelberg Catechism specifically. This book takes all of the questions and answers of the catechism and gives an exposition of them. Each section concludes with questions for study and discussion. I would recommend this book for daily devotional exercise. You will be introduced to the great themes of the faith in clear and concise language. The book, *The Heidelberg Catechism: A Study Guide* is published by Presbyterian and Reformed Publishers.

Dean Anderson Jr. writes in the forward to the book, "The value of the Heidelberg catechism is not restricted to one age or people, but insofar as it maps the saving doctrines of the Scriptures, it will be used with profit the world over."

Family Activity

There are many good catechisms that are available for you to use with your family. In addition, you can write your own catechism. Sit around the table with your family and create a catechism based on some of the things you have learned in this book.

Prayer

Lord help our family to grow in the wisdom and knowledge of Christ Jesus our Lord. Amen.

PART THREE

Theological Truths of the Reformation

Day Twenty Eight

Sin

*Scripture Reading: Psalm 51:3, John 8:7,
Romans 5:12; 6:23, I John 1:8*

The doctrine of sin was and is taken seriously by faithful adherents to Reformation theology. J. I. Packer notes that the Puritans viewed sin from the perspective of God's law, the Lordship of Christ and holiness. Sin was seen as transgression against God's law, rebellion against the Lordship of Christ and the corruption of holiness. (*A Quest for Godliness: The Puritan Vision of the Christian Life,* p. 29).

God created Adam and Eve upright and holy (Genesis 1:31). Adam stood as the representative of every person (Romans 5:12-21). We might say that the choices that Adam made in the Garden of Eden reflect the very choices that we would have made had we been actually been there. Adam was not only our representative. We are, in fact, his children because we have descended from him through his union with Eve. Originally Adam did not know sin by experience. However, Adam chose to willfully disobey the command of God and as a result brought the impact of sin not only on himself but on his posterity. We are born with a sin nature that is in need of deliverance from the chains of sin. We know that we are sinners because the Bible teaches that we are. We also know that we are sinners because of the choices that we make. We are not sinners because we sin— we sin because we are sinners. Our sin nature brings forth the wild fruit of unrighteousness. We are born in a fallen condition and we are helpless to rescue ourselves. Every part of us (intellect, emotions, and will) is fallen and in need of redemption. Left to ourselves, we will die in our sins and face eternal condemnation. Sin is rebellion against God.

Family Activity

Read the first two verses of Psalm 32. Find the words used for sin. In the New King James Version there are three words: transgression, sin and iniquity. Write those three words across the top of a sheet of paper. Beneath each word write a description. Transgression is rebellion against God. It means to leave the right way. Sin refers to missing the mark of God's law and His glory. Iniquity refers to that which is twisted, crooked or perverted. Sin is very serious.

Prayer

Lord help us to better understand the depth of our sin that we may repent and turn to You. Amen.

Day Twenty Nine

God

Scripture Reading: Genesis 1:1; Romans 5:8, 8:29-30

With the Reformation came a renewed vision of the greatness, majesty and glory of God. These were themes that were constantly preached, sung and written about. Christians were taught to consider God's glory in all of life and to live for His glory at work, play and during congregational worship. At the heart of Reformation theology was the glory of God in the salvation of sinners.

The Bible teaches that God is the Savior of sinners and that before He created the world, He set His love on His people in a unique way. There would be no hope for salvation from sin apart from God. The sinner is lost, fallen, blind and even dead spiritually. He cannot help Himself. He is in need of God to change His heart, forgive His sins and make him right with God.

The Bible teaches that God has chosen to do just that. God saves sinners and salvation is all to the glory of God (Read Ephesians 1-2).

Family Activity

What are some inappropriate ways that people often refer to God? Sometimes He is referred to as "the man upstairs." What are some other inappropriate expressions? Read Isaiah 6: 1-9 and Revelation 1:9-20. What picture emerges from those passages about God? Read also Isaiah 9:6-7 and Matthew 6:9. What do those passages teach about God? Learn the attributes of God and praise God for His character.

Prayer

Lord, You are glorious beyond compare. Your sovereign work in salvation is a marvelous display of Your glory. Thank You for being the Savior. Amen

Day Thirty

The Cross

Scripture Reading: Romans 8:31-39

The Bible teaches that God is holy and just. He cannot simply overlook our sins. Because He is so holy and sin is so wicked then sin must be punished for God's justice to be satisfied. God has chosen to make a way for sinners to be forgiven and made right with Him. That way is the way of the cross. The cross of Christ could have no impact for our salvation without the righteous life of Jesus. It is biblical to say that not only did Jesus *die* for sinners Jesus *lived* for sinners. Just as Adam stood as the representative of all of mankind, so Jesus stands as the representative of His people. Jesus gave His life for His church (Ephesians 5:25). The difference is that Adam failed. Jesus did not. Though Jesus was tempted as we are, He was without sin. Jesus willingly took the punishment for those that He came to save by voluntarily going to the cross. There the wrath of God was poured out on Him. God placed on His beloved Son the sin debt of His people. Jesus paid it all. God accepted the payment that Jesus made as is evidenced by the glorious resurrection of Jesus. Jesus lived, died, was buried and has risen from the dead. The only way to be delivered from sin is to repent and trust in Jesus Christ.

Family Activity

Today you will return to Psalm 32. Recently you read of the three words for sin in that passage. Today consider three words that portray forgiveness. They are found in verses one and two. Write the words "forgiven", "covered" and the phrase "does not impute iniquity" across the top of a page. Beneath "forgiven" write the word "unburdened." Sin is portrayed as a burden. Forgiveness is to have the burden of sin removed. John Bunyan in *The Pilgrim's Progress* describes the burden falling from the back of Christian and rolling down hill and into the grave. The word "covered" refers to the atonement. In the Old Testament the priest would take blood and sprinkle it on the mercy seat that covered the law of God in the Ark of the Covenant. The blood indicated that a sacrifice had been made for sin. If you are a Christian your sin has been covered by the death of Jesus Christ. The phrase "does not impute iniquity" refers to God not counting our sin against us because He counted our sin against Jesus who bore our punishment for us. This is why the Psalmist was so happy and wrote, "Blessed is he whose transgression is forgiven..." (Psalm 32:1). Augustine so loved this passage that it was inscribed in his bedroom so that as he died he could read of the blessedness of forgiveness.

Without the cross of Christ there is no forgiveness of sins. Because Jesus died on the cross there is substantive hope for all who will trust in Him.

Prayer

Lord thank You for the cross and the amazing love that the death of Jesus displayed there. Thank You for the blessing of forgiveness. Please search our hearts and help us to discern whether or not we are Christians. If so help us to better praise You. If not then open our hearts to receive the message of the cross. Amen.

Day Thirty-One

Holy Spirit

Scripture Reading: John 16:7-13

How can a lost and blind sinner repent and believe? The answer is found in the work of the Holy Spirit. The Bible says that we "must be born again" (John 3:7). That refers to the new birth. According to the Bible this birth is not by man's will but God's and it is Spirit induced (John 1:11-13; John 3:1-8). The Holy Spirit brings the dead sinner to life, gives him a new heart with new desires for God, and calls that sinner to come to Christ. The sinner then repents of sin and trusts God to save him by Christ. Christians should be faithful to call people to come to Christ. However, it is the Holy Spirit who issues an internal call resulting in those chosen by God actually coming to Christ. The Holy Spirit brings lost people to life, calls them to Christ and grants them repentance and faith. He then comes to live in the life of the Christian.

The Holy Spirit is God, the third member of the Trinity. The Bible was inspired by the Spirit; the Holy Spirit convicts the sinner of his sin; the Holy

Spirit brings the dead sinner to life; and the Holy Spirit indwells the believer.

Family Activity

Take a Bible concordance and look up references to the Holy Spirit. Take a sheet of paper and write down some of the things that you learn about the Spirit. Remember that the Holy Spirit is a person. It is not appropriate to refer to the Holy Spirit as an "it." The Holy Spirit is a "He."

Prayer

Lord thank You for the ministry of the Holy Spirit. We acknowledge His deity and His work in bringing sinners to the Savior. Amen.

Day Thirty-Two

Preservation

Scripture Reading: John 5:24, Romans 8:1-11

When God saves a sinner He sends His Holy Spirit to live inside of them. The Holy Spirit preserves the Christian so that he will never be lost. The Spirit enables the Christian to persevere in the faith. The Believer has new desires and therefore seeks to be faithful to God. This is one of the great works of the Spirit in the heart of those that God has saved.

The love of God is evident in preserving those that He saves. Salvation is referred to as "everlasting life" (John 3:16). Romans chapter eight and verse thirty gives us a sweeping picture of God's preserving work in the life of His child. First He predestines, then He calls, next He justifies and finally he glorifies His children. If this were pictured as a chain then there are no broken links. Those that God chooses He promises to make holy and take them to heaven. This is a very comforting doctrine that encourages Christians to be faithful.

Family Activity

Today you may have encountered some biblical terms that you are not familiar with. It would be helpful to have a Bible dictionary to help your children better grasp these terms. Have your children either make or draw a picture of a chain. In each link write one of the words from Romans 8:30. Though your paper chain might be broken there is no breakage in the chain of God's redeeming work on behalf of His children.

Prayer

Lord thank You that by Your Spirit salvation is secure. Please produce a heart of love and thankfulness for and to You for your wonderful work of salvation. Thank You for never forsaking Your people. Amen.

Day Thirty Three

The Reformation and the Five Points

Scripture Reading: John 6:44, 10:15; Romans 3:9-18,25; 9:14-18; 2 Timothy 2:11-12

As the Reformation spread, it was met with opposition from the Roman church and also from professing Christians that did not hold to Reformation theology. One group of opponents to the teaching of Luther, Calvin and Zwingli was inspired by the teaching and writings of a man by the name of Jacob Arminius (1559-1609). Arminius believed that God saves those that He knows will come to faith in Him. The emphasis was on the will of man over and above the will of God. The followers of Arminius were called Arminians. After Arminius died his followers protested the doctrine of the Reformers. They made their protest in the form of five points. The Arminians believed that God's election of people to salvation was conditioned upon their future faith. They also believed that the death of Christ made salvation a possibility but that it did not guarantee the salvation of anyone. They believed that just as a person may choose to come to Christ on their own, they may also choose to leave Christ and therefore fall from grace.

The Reformers responded with five points of their own. The teaching of the Reformers is often communicated by the acronym TULIP. Though TULIP was not created by Calvin, Luther or Zwingli it nevertheless expresses the heart of their teaching on salvation.

Total Depravity This point deals with the sin of man. Every part of man has been radically impacted by sin, so that it is proper to say that though a person does not commit all of the sins that they are capable of committing, they are nonetheless without ability to please God.

Unconditional Election This phrase points to the sovereignty of God. Since no one has a natural ability to please God and if left to themselves they will die outside of Christ, God chooses to set His special love on His people in such a way that will result in them coming to Christ.

Limited Atonement This speaks to the design of the death of Christ. Though the death of Christ is sufficient to cover all of the sins of every person who has, does and will ever exist, it is designed to pay in full the sin-debt of those that God has chosen to elect to salvation. The atonement of Christ *actually* and not just *potentially* paid for the sins of those that God elected to save.

Irresistible Grace This refers to the fact that when God saves a sinner He changes his heart and the sinner who once was rebellious to God is changed to love the Lord. Therefore, the sinner willingly comes to God by faith in Jesus Christ.

Perseverance of the Saints This doctrine proclaims the good news that those whom God saves He keeps so that they will never fall from their salvation.

Family Activity

TULIP has often been referred to as "Calvinism." Though John Calvin certainly believed the teachings that TULIP communicates, he taught many other things. The focus of Calvin was on the supremacy and sovereignty of God. This he learned from reading the Apostle Paul and also from reading Augustine. Calvinism is a world-view that sees all of life through the lens of God's glory. Whether you agree or disagree with all of the points of TULIP it is important to understand the theology of TULIP. Many Christian leaders in history such as George Whitfield, Jonathan Edwards and Charles Spurgeon were "Calvinists." There are many Christian pastors today who believe TULIP, men such as John Piper, John MacArthur, R.C. Sproul, Ligon Duncan, Albert Mohler and many others. The Southern Baptist Convention, in its early days, was lead by men who were Calvinistic in their theology, men like John Dagg, Basil Manly, J.P. Boyce and John Broadus.

Though you may or may not be Calvinistic in your theology, help your children to understand the doctrines and to appreciate those evangelistic Christians in history who were Calvinists. Perhaps the words of the famous Baptist Charles Spurgeon are helpful for us at this point: "I am never ashamed to avow myself a Calvinist; I do not hesitate to take the name of Baptist; but if asked what is my creed, I reply, 'it is Jesus Christ'."

Take some paper and draw a picture of a tulip. Write a point of TULIP on each petal. Beneath the flower write the names of faithful Christians throughout history who have loved and taught TULIP (sometimes referred to as the doctrines of grace). Though there are distinctions between the Reformers you will find that most agreed with TULIP. Though this is a challenging and sometimes controversial subject we should search the Scriptures to discover the truth and to love all people who love the Lord Jesus.

Prayer

Lord thank You for being a wonderful Savior. Thank You that though we have sinned, in Your power and grace You have provided salvation through the death of Your Son. Help us to be God-centered in our theology and loving towards our brothers and sisters in Christ. Amen.

Day Thirty Four

Five Strong Stones

Scripture Reading: Joshua 4:21; Ephesians 1-2

The Reformation produced a number of memorable phrases that are strong stones upon which we can stand on and cling to.

Sola Scriptura Martin Luther discovered that ultimate authority did not rest in popes or councils of church leaders. Ultimate authority rests with God as revealed in his infallible (without ability to err), inspired (God-breathed), inerrant (without error), sufficient (all that we need to know and live for God) word—the Bible.

Sola Fide As Luther studied the books of Romans and Galatians he uncovered the great truth that salvation is by faith in Jesus Christ and not by the works of man.

Sola Gratia Salvation by faith in Christ is possible only because of the grace of God given to His elect that they might repent and believe in Christ. Salvation is by grace alone, through faith alone.

Sola Christus God's grace changes the heart of a person leading them to place faith in Christ alone for salvation. Salvation is by grace alone, through faith alone, in Christ alone, according to the Scripture alone.

Soli Deo Gloria Why does God save a sinner from their sins? He saves the sinner for His own glory. From beginning to end salvation is a gracious gift from a benevolent God and therefore God alone is to receive glory (Ephesians 1:3-14).

Family Activity

Gather five large rocks and clean them up. Write the reformation "solas" on them and explain what they mean. You will have a permanent reminder of some of the most important teachings of the Reformation. These stones can be displayed in your home. Perhaps your grandchildren will one day ask about the meaning of the stones.

Prayer

Lord You have given us a strong biblical foundation on which we can stand. We acknowledge that salvation is by grace alone, through faith alone, in Christ alone, according to Scripture alone and to Your glory alone. Help us to be careful to teach salvation by grace. Amen.

Day Thirty-Five

The Chief End of Man

Scripture Reading: I Corinthians 10:31

What is the chief end of man? The chief end of man is to glorify God and to enjoy Him forever. This is the first question and answer of the Westminster shorter catechism developed at Westminster Abbey by some of the godliest ministers of the day.

The answer to this question is a good summary of the teaching and reason for the Reformation. Above all else, the Reformation was about ascribing glory to God and glorifying Him through a life of finding ultimate joy in Christ.

The Reformation was a Bible movement. During those days, the Bible was dusted off, read, studied and made available to the common man. God's Word, which cannot be bound, was unleashed afresh and the wildfires of revival and reform touched Germany, Scotland, Switzerland, England, the Netherlands and the New World.

There are great lessons from the Reformation for us as individuals and our churches. Let us read, study, teach, and preach the Bible. Let us not hide from our children the lessons of history (Psalm 78:1-7).

Family Activity

Create a little test for your family. Ask questions about the key characters and themes of the Reformation. Use illustrations such as five stones or the tulip and have them write on the stones and flower doctrines that were rediscovered during the Reformation.

Prayer

Lord thank You for the lessons that we have learned in the past thirty-five days. As we have studied the lives and teachings of courageous men and women help us to remember that You are the hero of history. To You alone be glory. Amen.

PART FOUR
Final Helps and Thoughts

Character Sketches

Here is a brief list of a few characters of the Reformation. Some are included in the daily reading of the book but others are not. Make your own list from your daily readings, the list below and other biographical studies.

Amman - Jacob Amman led many pilgrims to break ties with the world and to live simple lives. He also promoted religious liberty from the government. His followers are called the Amish today.

Beza - Theodore Beza was a scholar and friend of Calvin who published an edition of the Greek New Testament and sought reforms and freedom of religion in France. He helped to cement the ideas of Calvin for future generations.

Bradstreet - Anne Bradstreet was a Puritan who wrote poetry that encouraged the church and was one of the many women who helped shape Reformation teaching on family life.

Bunyan - John Bunyan was a Puritan preacher who was jailed after the death of Oliver Cromwell. He is most famous for writing the allegory *The Pilgrim's Progress*.

Calvin - John Calvin is most known for TULIP. TULIP is an acrostic that summarizes Reformation theology. This acrostic was not developed by Calvin but was a later attempt to explain some of what he taught. Calvin helped Christians to develop a more biblical understanding of the church and a God-centered worldview.

Cranmer - Thomas Cranmer was a minister for Henry VIII and was a key figure in the English Reformation. He authored articles of faith, a prayer book and worked at reforming the practice of worship services. Cranmer was very influential in the reign of Henry VIII's son, Edward VI. He was burned at the stake.

Cromwell - Oliver Cromwell became the ruler of England in the 1650's and filled the parliament with Puritans. He enacted laws with biblical values and allowed Puritans to preach freely.

Foxe - John Foxe wrote *Foxe's Book of Martyrs* to tell the stories of heroes who were martyred for their faith. His purpose in writing this historic book was to encourage Christians to remain steadfast in the face of persecution.

Grebel - Conrad Grebel baptized George Blaurock by immersion in 1524. He and other Anabaptists believed that the Bible taught baptism was only for Christians. Everyone who was baptized by immersion faced danger from both Reformed and Catholic authorities.

Henry VIII - Henry VIII declared himself the head of the Church of England because the pope refused to allow him a divorce from his wife Elizabeth. He said he wanted to rid England of Catholicism, but mostly he was motivated by self interest.

Hus - Jan Hus was a priest in Bohemia. He desired a Bible in the language of the people, led his church congregation to sing together and preached from the Bible. He was martyred in 1415 because of these practices.

Knox - John Knox established the Presbyterian Church and laid out three principles to mark the true church: the preaching of the word, correct practice of the sacraments, and church discipline. He launched a massive education campaign designed to teach everyone in Scotland to read.

Latimer - Hugh Latimer was burned at the stake for his beliefs and told his friend who was burned with him, "Be of good comfort Mr. Ridley, and play the man. We shall this day light a candle by God's grace, in England, as I trust never shall be put out."

Luther - Martin Luther nailed the 95 theses to the church door to help the pope understand, among other things, the financial abuses of some church leaders like Tetzel. The pope sided against Luther. Martin Luther was excommunicated from the Catholic Church. He taught key doctrines of the Protestant church summarized by the five *solas*.

Mary - Queen Mary was the daughter of Henry VIII who sought to bring back Catholicism to England. She murdered hundreds of Protestants. She is known as Bloody Mary.

Muentzer - Thomas Muentzer led the peasants' revolt against the Church and the authority it held over common people. He was beheaded in 1525.

Puritans - Puritans were reformers who sought a pure church and life. Many of them left England to pursue religious liberty in the Netherlands and the New World (United States). Jonathan Edwards was an heir of the Puritans.

Sattler - Michael Sattler taught against infant baptism, the pope's authority and Christ's body being present at communion. He was tortured and burned at the stake in 1527.

Simons - Menno Simons believed that Christians should separate themselves from political and governmental involvement and was committed to nonviolence. The Mennonites were those who followed the teachings of Simons.

Von Bora - Katharina von Bora was a nun who, along with other nuns, escaped a convent by hiding in a fish barrel. The nuns wanted to meet Martin Luther. Katharina married Luther. She gave birth to six children, and she and Martin adopted six more children. Luther called her "Katy, my rib."

Waldo - Peter Waldo was one of the first men to translate the Bible into French and establish a dedicated group of preachers of the gospel. He lived during the 1100's.

Wycliffe - John Wycliffe oversaw the translating of the Bible into English and taught against the corruption in the Catholic Church. He died in 1384 but his body was later dug up and burned because of his teachings.

Zwingli - Ulrich Zwingli preached against Catholic Church practices. He brought the Reformation to Switzerland and founded a school that taught the Bible in its original languages. He preached to the people in their own language.

The Reformation for Today

Though almost five hundred years separate us from the Protestant Reformation the truths rediscovered during that time are timeless.

The true nature of the church and the importance of congregational and family life were emphasized during the Reformation. Today congregational identity is often considered optional at best and unnecessary at worst. The Reformation reminds us that godly churches are marked by biblical preaching, participation in the ordinances (or sacraments), church discipline and biblical fellowship.

In our modern families that are often scattered and broken the Reformation teaches us that the home is a "little church" where Christ is to be worshiped.

What are some of the practical truths that will help to cultivate reformation in our churches and homes today?

1. Supplication.

   Amidst all of the mediators promoted by the Catholic Church in the sixteenth century, Martin Luther was, by God's grace, able to strip away the layers of church tradition and dust off I Timothy 2:5. *For there is one God and one Mediator between God and men, the Man Christ Jesus.* Christ alone is the Mediator between God and man—not the church, not a venerated Saint from the past, not the pope but Christ (John 14:6). Prayer, then, is directed to God by faith in Jesus Christ. Through Christ the Christian comes confidently to God in expectation that God will hear and answer prayer (Hebrews 4:16). When David sought reform and renewal he did so by means of prayer (Psalm 119:25). Local congregations, seeking reform, should pray.

2. Scripture

In the years prior to Luther's nailing of the 95 theses to the church door, the pre-Reformation was at work in men like John Wycliffe (1320-1384). Wycliffe labored to put the Bible into the language of the people. He took his translation from the Latin Vulgate and in the 1380's his handwritten manuscript of the Bible in English was available.

The printing press would come along 100 years later and William Tyndale's work would be more widely distributed. William Tyndale (1494-1536) relied on the Hebrew and Greek text as the foundation for his Bible translation. He was much opposed and ultimately imprisoned and martyred for his faith and work. His spirit is reflective of all of the faithful Protestant Reformers. Catholic leaders sought to keep the Bible out of reach for the common person. The result was that non-biblical teachings supplanted the Scripture in the lives of the people. The Roman Church became increasingly powerful and corrupt and saw itself as the determiner of what people should know and believe. It was, in essence, the Church alone rather than *sola scriptura*, Scripture alone. Tyndale's desire was to translate the Bible into English. One church leader intimated that it would be better for the people to be without the law of God than without the law of the pope. Tyndale's famous response was: "...if God spares my life, I will cause the English plow boy to know more of the Scriptures than the pope himself."

Around 1526 Tyndale's New Testament was complete. Tyndale would later be betrayed, cast into prison and ultimately burned at the stake. However, he knew that "the word of God is not chained" (2 Timothy 2:9). The martyrdom of Tyndale was used for good by God. The Bible was more widely distributed and even placed into the pulpits of England by the king's command.

During the time of the Reformation preaching was restored to the pulpit, the Bible was returned to the people and the foundation for family worship was reestablished. The Puritans would stand on the Reformer's work and leave a legacy of rich preaching and writing about God, the church and the home.

For Reform to come to our local churches and in our families then we must be a people of the Bible

Bible reading, biblical preaching and family worship are essential to modern day reform. When David prayed for revival he was confident that true revival comes by the Word of God. *"My soul clings to the dust; Revive me according to Your word" (Psalm 119:25)*

3. Singing

The Reformation gave to the church a renewed emphasis on congregational singing. Luther wrote songs that were God-centered and Scripture saturated. It is difficult for us to imagine a church service without singing but for many years, prior to the Reformation, congregational singing was absent from the church. This was an evidence of a church smothered by arrogant church leadership in which the people were not trusted with either the Word or song. We are in line with the Reformers when we ask the question, "What does the Bible teach about church music?"

The Bible commands us to "be filled with the Spirit" (Ephesians 5:18) with the resulting action in the following verse, "speaking to one another in psalms and hymns and spiritual songs, singing and making melody in your heart to the Lord." "Let the word of Christ dwell in you richly in all wisdom, teaching and admonishing one another in psalms and hymns and spiritual songs, singing with grace in your hearts to the Lord" (Colossians 3:16). These passages were written to local churches and the emphasis was on congregational singing.

When we gather with our church family we should sing. Singing should be the overflow of a heart that is "filled with the Spirit" because the "word of Christ" dwells in us. Singing then is Spirit-filled, Christ-centered, biblically driven and edifying to others. Questions we should ask in our congregational singing include:
Are the songs saturated with Scripture? This means more than simply a Bible verse repeated over and over but is reflective of all of the "word of Christ."

Are the songs edifying to others? The best songs in Christian history are instructive. A very powerful way to remember truth is to sing truth. Truth set to music is not only edifying but also reflects a congregation's commitment to *sola Scriptura.* Church leaders should consider what Christian truths are taught by the songs that are chosen for corporate worship.

Congregational life calls on us to be considerate of one another (Hebrews 10:24-25). Too often the young person is pitted against the old or the old against the young. Sometimes the church is divided up into several different "worship" services on the

Lord's Day. This division is often related to music. The Bible calls upon us to think of ourselves as members of a family with fathers and mothers and sisters and brothers and sons and daughters (I Timothy 5).

Godly content communicated by consistent music is essential in good congregational singing. However, we must guard against establishing personal preferences as church law when it comes to singing and music. The young people of the church should be taught to appreciate the time-tested and God-centered music written hundreds of years ago. The older people of the church should be encouraged to appreciate modern songs that reflect a biblical perspective.

Do the songs reflect heart love for Christ? Singing, like any other aspect of congregational worship, can be duty driven rather than delight driven. Of course singing is a Christian duty, but it is not a cold, formal duty that is isolated from deep affection for God. We should come to church repentantly and sing joyfully.

Supplication, Scripture and singing are legitimate areas for reform in our churches and families. Let us seek God in repentant prayer, saturate our hearts with Scripture and rise up to sing His praises.

Helps and Discussion Starters

The information below includes some discussion starters, terms you may want to familiarize yourself with and other thoughts.

1. What is the providence of God? You can expand your answer by using a good systematic theology or theological dictionary.
2. What does the term "Reformation" mean? What is reformation theology as used in this book?
3. What is a monastery? What is a monk?
4. What is a pope? What is Saint Peter's Cathedral?
5. What were the Crusades?
6. What are indulgences?
7. What is the Catholic doctrine of purgatory?
8. What are treasuries of merit that the church claimed to control?
9. What is the mass?
10. What is the Castle Church in Wittenberg?
11. During the Reformation what was significant about the Wartburg Castle?
12. Who was Augustine? The Reformers relied heavily on the teaching of Augustine. You may want to read Augustine's *Confessions*.

13. Do a study on the New Testament books of *Galatians* and *Romans*.
14. This book will give you a great opportunity to add some geographical material to your library. Make sure that you have a variety of maps available.
15. What plague came to Zurich during the days of Zwingli that resulted in the death of 2,000 people?
16. What is a parish?
17. What is a Commonwealth?
18. Who was Oliver Cromwell and by what title is he remembered?
19. What are "The Institutes of the Christian Religion?"
20. What is a confession of faith?

Materials List

The following materials will be helpful in using this book.

Paper, pencils and whiteboard for various days

Dictionary (Webster's and theological-see bibliography) and a notebook to record unfamiliar terms that you should define.

Blank journal – day 1

A copy of an important document such as a birth certificate – day 5

Globe – day 6, 9, 12, 24

Profiles in Courage by John F. Kennedy – available at the library - day 11

Bible concordance – day 13

L'Abri by Edith Schaffer – day 16

A copy of a church bulletin – day 22

Several translations of the Bible – day 23

Pilgrim's Progress by John Bunyan in an easy to read children's version (see bibliography) – day 25

Variety of catechisms – day 27

Consider adding to your library a copy of the *Westminster Confession of Faith, The Heidelberg Catechism, The Belgic Confession, the Canons of Dordt, the 1689 Second London Baptist Confession of Faith.*

Five large rocks or stones – day 34

Reformation era books, history books and pictures.

Annotated Bibliography

Bainton, Roland H. *The Reformation of the Sixteenth Century*, Boston, Beacon 1952. 278p. *Brief but thorough introduction to the Reformation.*

Bunyan, John. *The Pilgrim's Progress*, Edinburgh, Banner of Truth, 1977. 379p. *This is one of many good editions of one of the greatest books in history.*

Houghton, Sidney Maurice. *Sketches from Church History: An Illustrated Account of 20 Centuries of Christ's Power.* Edinburgh, The Banner of Truth Trust, 1980. 256p. *The title of this volume tells the story. This book should be in your home library.*

Hunkin, Oliver. *The Dangerous Journey*, Grand Rapids, Eerdmans, 1985. 126p. *Perhaps the best children's abridgment of "Pilgrim's Progress" available. Beautifully illustrated. Our younger children have spent hours looking at the illustrations in this book.*

Kleyn, Diana. with Beeke, Joel. *Reformation Heroes*, Grand Rapids, MI: Reformation Heritage, 2007. 240p. *Helpful book that is filled with Reformation era character sketches and contains many lovely illustrations.*

Newton, Richard. *Heroes of the Reformation: Life-Changing Lessons for the Young*, Vestavia Hills, AL., Solid Ground Christian Books, 2005, 273p. *Wonderful book written by "The prince of preachers to children" but helpful to young and old alike. Visit the web-site of Solid Ground Christian Books for a number of helpful resources on the Reformation and other books by Richard Newton.*

Foxe, John. *The New Foxe's Book of Martyrs*, Alachua, FL., Bridge Logos., 2001, 491p. *Foxe's Book of Martyrs is a must for every library.*

Godfrey, Robert W., *Reformation Sketches*, Phillipsburg., P&R, 2003, 151p. *Robert Godfrey is an outstanding preacher and writer. This is a great introduction to some of the key Reformation characters and literature.*

Grenz, S., D. Guretzki, and C.F. Nordling. *Pocket Dictionary of Theological Terms.* IVP, 1999. 122p. *Helpful book of concise definitions to theological terms.*

Grudem, Wayne. *Bible Doctrine: Essential Teachings of the Christian Faith*, Grand Rapids, Zondervan. 1999. 528p. *This would be a helpful volume to have by your side as you work through the family worship book.*

Nichols, Stephen. *The Reformation: how a monk and a mallet changed the world.* Wheaton, Crossway Books, 2007. 159p. *Stephen Nichols is an outstanding writer. This is a lively introduction to the Reformation and highly recommended.*

Packer, J.I., *A Quest for Godliness: The Puritan Vision of the Christian Life*, Wheaton, Crossway, 1990. 367p. *This is one of my all time favorite books. It is now available in paperback.*

Shelley, Bruce, L. *Church History in Plain Language*, 2nd ed. Nashville, Thomas Nelson, 1995. 528p. *Interesting and easy to read history book that is not dry and does not bog down.*

Van Dyken, Donald. *Rediscovering Catechism: The Art of Equipping Covenant Children*, P & R Publishing, Phillipsburg, P & R, 2000. 146p. *I found this to be a very helpful guide in understanding the why and how of catechisms.*

Williamson, G. I. *The Heidelberg Catechism: A Study Guide*, Phillipsburg: P&R Publishing, 1993. 241p. *This is a good tool for understanding and using the Heidelberg Catechism.*

About the Author

Ray Rhodes, Jr. is President of Nourished in the Word Ministries. Nourished in the Word is a teaching, writing and church planting ministry. Ray and Lori have been married for over 20 years and are blessed with five daughters: Rachel, Hannah, Sarah, Mary and Lydia. To schedule Ray to speak for your next event, please contact him at ray@nourishedintheword.org. Lori is available to speak to ladies groups on a variety of issues related to godly womanhood. Visit Lori on the web at www.nitw4ladies.blogspot.com

Ray and his family live in North Georgia.

Family Worship for the Christmas Season
by Ray Rhodes, Jr.

"Ray Rhodes has written a wonderfully creative book on family worship for the Christmas season. For a father or mother to take their children through these precious truths would create a fond memory that the children would have for the rest of their life. The book is doctrinally sound, well written, and greatly honoring to our Lord. I'm going to order three copies right now!"
- **Martha Peace,** Biblical Counselor and author of *The Excellent Wife*

"The Christmas season is a great time for daily family worship. If you've never enjoyed family worship on a consistent basis, there's no better time to start. Whether your family already enjoys the biblical and historic Christian practice of family worship or you're just beginning, consider using Ray Rhodes' engaging *Family Worship for the Christmas Season* this December."
- **Dr. Donald S. Whitney**, author of *Spiritual Disciplines of the Christian Life*

"The Incarnation of Jesus Christ is one of the most important events in the history of the world. Too many years families get so tangled in the trappings of Christmas, however, that they miss its true wonder. Ray Rhodes has written a wonderful book that elegantly encourages and practically helps families draw near to each another as they draw near to the Lord in celebrating his birth. I highly recommend it."
- **John Crotts**, pastor and author of *Mighty Men: the Starter's Guide to Leading Your Family*

Call us at **1-866-789-7423**
Visit us at **www.solid-ground-books.com**

OTHER SGCB TITLES FOR THE FAMILY

In addition to the title in your hands we are delighted to offer several other titles from Solid Ground Christian Books for the family. Here is a sample:

Little Pillows and Morning Bells by Francis Havergal
The Child's Book on the Fall by Thomas H Gallaudet
The Child's Book on the Soul by T.H. Gallaudet
The Child's Book of Natural Theology by Gallaudet
The Child's Book on the Sabbath by Horace Hooker
Feed My Lambs by John Todd
Truth Made Simple by John Todd
The Tract Primer by the American Tract Society
The Child at Home by John S.C. Abbott
Early Piety Illustrated by Gorham Abbott
Repentance & Faith for the Young by Charles Walker
Jesus the Way by Edward Payson Hammond
The Pastor's Daughter by Louisa Payson Hopkins
Lectures on the Bible to the Young by John Eadie
The Scripture Guide by James W. Alexander
My Brother's Keeper by James W. Alexander
The Chief End of Man by John Hall
Old Paths for Little Feet by Carol Brandt
Small Talks on Big Questions by Selah Helms
Advice to a Young Christian by Jared Waterbury
Bible Promises by Richard Newton
Bible Warnings by Richard Newton
Bible Models by Richard Newton
Bible Animals by Richard Newton
Bible Jewels by Richard Newton
Heroes of the Early Church by Richard Newton
Heroes of the Reformation by Richard Newton
Safe Compass and How it Points by Richard Newton
The King's Highway by Richard Newton
The Life of Jesus Christ for the Young by Newton
Rays from the Sun of Righteousness by Newton

Call us Toll Free at **1-866-789-7423**
Visit us on-line at **www.solid-ground-books.com**